BOMBSITES
&
LOLLIPOPS

JACKY HYAMS

BOMBSITES & LOLLIPOPS

My 1950s East End Childhood

JOHN BLAKE

Published by John Blake Publishing Ltd,
3 Bramber Court, 2 Bramber Road,
London W14 9PB, England

www.johnblakepublishing.co.uk

www.facebook.com/johnblakebooks ⬜
twitter.com/jblakebooks ⬜

First published in paperback in 2011

ISBN: 978 1 84358 352 3

British Library Cataloguing-in-Publication Data:

A catalogue record for this book is available from the British Library.

Design by www.envydesign.co.uk

Printed in Great Britain by CPI Group (UK) Ltd

5 7 9 10 8 6 4

Papers used by John Blake Publishing are natural, recyclable products made from
wood grown in sustainable forests. The manufacturing processes conform to the
environmental regulations of the country of origin.

Every attempt has been made to contact the relevant copyright-holders, but some
were unobtainable. We would be grateful if the appropriate people could contact us.
people could contact us.

ABOUT THE AUTHOR

Jacky Hyams is a freelance journalist, author and former magazine editor who has written extensively on a wide range of topics for many leading publications in the UK and Australia. Her work has appeared in *Cosmopolitan, Rolling Stone, New Idea, Cleo, The Sydney Morning Herald, The Evening Standard, The Times, Daily Mirror, Daily Star, Sunday Express, Best, Bella, Now, Woman's Own, Hello, What's On TV, Woman & Home, Woman's Weekly* and many other publications. She lives in West Hampstead, London.

FOREWORD

All gratitude to Wensley Clarkson for encouraging me to venture into my past in the first place and helping me understand that the journey may be daunting – but is well worth taking.

Most sincere thanks to Tammy Cohen, for her friendship and valuable support and to my dear and lifelong friend Larraine De Napoli, who was generous with her time and patience in sharing her recollections of our teenage years.

Thanks too to John Parrish in Sydney, who never fails to support and inspire from a great distance with wry humour and insight.

I'd also like to pass on my thanks to everyone on the team at the Hackney Archive for their helpful advice and enthusiasm.

Finally, three classic historical sources which have proved invaluable:

- *London 1945* by Maureen Waller;
- *Austerity Britain, 1945-1951* by David Kynaston;
- *Family Britain, 1951-1957* by David Kynaston.

CONTENTS

Introduction   ix
1   The Vicar's Baby   1
2   A Telegram   5
3   A Homecoming   15
4   Bets Are On   26
5   Neighbours   34
6   Sundays   43
7   A Liberty Bodice   53
8   The Ascot's Revenge   60
9   A Diamond Ring   65
10 A Rat's Tale   75
11 A Piano   83
12 Farthings   90
13 A Wedding   98
14 School Milk   108
15 Beside the Sea…   113
16 The Good Friday Agreement   119

17 The Elvis Years   128
18 One Night of Shame   136
19 The Ideal Home   144
20 An Ending   153
21 First Kiss   163
22 The Apprentice   176
23 Party with the Kray Twins   188
24 Working Girl   195
25 A Stunt   202
26 What's in the Box?   207
27 A Ferry Ride   219
28 A Plan   230
29 She's Leaving Home…   235
Afterwards   240

INTRODUCTION

3am: Saturday, 27 September 2008
The bedside light clicks on. Wide awake. Again. Another broken night's sleep. If I read for an hour or so, maybe slumber will return. Reaching out for the pile of unread newspapers by the bed, I pluck a colour supplement from the top of the pile and turn to the first page.

And I can't quite believe what I'm seeing.

For my weary eye has been instantly drawn to a black-and-white photo in the middle of the page.

It is a powerful image, used to illustrate a historical feature in the *Financial Times* weekend magazine: a throng of City gents at the London Stock Exchange reading the latest newspapers, a fly-on-the-wall reaction shot taken by a *Daily Express* photographer.

And the news that day in 1938 was both dramatic and momentous. Britain's Prime Minister, Neville Chamberlain, had returned from a brief visit to Munich to tell the world he'd reached an agreement with Hitler: we would not go to war with Germany.

It was a misleading about-turn in history, an all-too-brief moment of hope, a bleak false dawn that would unravel within twelve months.

Yet it is the pretty young woman at the very centre of the crowd, looking directly at the camera, who really makes the photo come to life. She's smartly attired: a neat tailored suit, pendant around her neck, jaunty little black hat. And she's smiling, a youthful smile that somehow embodies the brief optimism of the hour. Close by, a fresh-faced young man with round glasses and wavy hair looks startled, unsure of what's happening. Somehow the photographer has managed to capture the emotional timbre of the times.

I stare at the photo in total shock, because the youthful

couple are my parents, Molly and Ginger, in their courting days, long before I arrived on the scene. I have many black-and-white photos of them after their marriage a few years later. And I will never know what they were doing at the Stock Exchange that historic night. But I had never seen my parents as they were then: so young, so vulnerable, unaware of the mayhem that lay ahead.

What makes the image doubly poignant, however, is the contrast with the present. For the pretty young girl in the picture is now a very frail, confused ninety-two-year-old living in a care home, totally dependent on the support of others. I had visited her hours before, made her a cup of tea and smoothed scented cream onto her wrinkled hands. And although I can't quite bring myself to acknowledge it right now, her life is slowly ebbing away.

Although I'm excited at having discovered this amazing archive photo in such a random way – I might easily have left the supplement unopened, as happens sometimes with the weekend papers – I am somewhat perplexed at the timing. Why now? Always slightly superstitious, searching for hidden meaning, once I have contacted Getty Images, the photographic archive credited, and confirmed that I can buy my own copy of the photo, I start to wonder: are my parents trying to reach out to me in some way? My dad had died decades before. As for my mother, when I do show her the photo a few days later she does not react in any way. She can't. Her memory is virtually gone, though thankfully she holds fast to her recognition of me. To her, it's just a piece of paper. She feels no identifiable relationship with the pretty young girl with the bright smile.

But what are they trying to say, waving at me from the distance of so many decades?

Do they want me to remember their times, what they lived through, how it was for them after the photo was taken, when they and millions of others were plunged headlong into the chaos of World War II?

Or are they merely trying to reassure me, let me know that somehow, they are watching me, looking out for me? This, of course, is a pleasant and comforting thought. But I do not hold any religious beliefs. Nor did my parents. I have long held a half-formed belief that there may be spiritual worlds out there that we don't quite understand, can't readily access. My mother too was acutely aware of such things. After my dad died she'd fallen seriously ill. 'He was trying to take me with him,' she told me afterwards.

But when I rationalise it, ask myself for the umpteenth time why this photo should fall into my hands now, of course I can't quite reach any coherent answer. The journalist in me is gratified to see my parents' image captured at such a significant moment in London's long history. That will have to do.

Less than a year later, my mother is gone, swiftly and without fuss, after lunch on a summer's day. It shouldn't have been a shock, but it turns my world upside down. Our bonds have always been very close, drawn even closer since she became so frail and needy. So I don't get round to collecting the framed Getty image until months afterwards.

But finally, once it has been carefully hung on my bedroom wall, I start to understand what the image means for me: it's up to me to tell their story, as I know it, not the history of their respective families or everything that happened to them during their lives, but the story of my childhood, growing up with them in London's East End after peace had been declared; my own snapshot, if you like, of two decades that were so very different from the world we now live in.

Naturally, I hesitate. It's not exactly thrilling when you realise that your own life is history, you've been around so long that many of your references are unrecognisable, unknown to many. And it's daunting too because mine was not a joyful childhood, though I'm conscious that I am not alone in this. Do I really want to go there? Should I reach out to exhume the bad moments, the tears, the confusion? They're not exactly buried deep. So why rake over what is done? After all, I was fortunate; I never knew want or need. And while my relationship with my father was wrecked by his relationship with alcohol and I grew to loathe our environment, my mother was as loving a parent as anyone could ever wish for. Moreover, my subsequent life as a globe-trotting journalist and writer has proved to be as exciting and varied as anyone might desire.

But while I was born into a black-and-white world where people shivered and could only dream of an era of blue skies and well-stocked larders, I realise that there was colour too in the emerging post-war world. It might not have been instantly visible. But step by step, huge emerging social reforms were to transform lives in ways that would have been unimaginable at the time that photo was taken: free healthcare and education for all, the abolition of hanging, the arrival of the contraceptive pill, the reforms to divorce and abortion laws, the legalisation of homosexuality. Decades of making do – rationing didn't finally end until 1954 – gave way to full employment, cheap foreign travel, consumer goods for all. It's a story worth telling for more than personal reasons.

OK, so it was a bizarre childhood in many ways, living in a bomb-scarred street in Hackney with a dad whose wallet was permanently stuffed with notes. But as a child then, you only knew one world, your own streets, the lives around you. You weren't bombarded, 24/7 with incessant images of other, far more glamorous lives of luxury, endless partying and permanent sunshine, where only fame itself must be sought to achieve the perfect life. I never knew envy or aspiration simply because I didn't see much that was different or distracting to envy. I took our upside-down world for granted: an abundance of food and black-market goodies; being driven around by a chauffeur in a Daimler, smartly turned out like a little princess with a glamorous mum.

Any fear I might have known existed mainly in my imagination, though being an overprotected child created a curious mix of physical timidity with a somewhat verbose confidence. And whatever the shortcomings of my immediate world, I easily found my escape through the written word: stifling and claustrophobic as the backdrop of childhood was, writing was my key to a future as yet undreamed of.

So this is my story of those years, of that lost world. Apprehensive when I sat down to start writing it, as the memoir grew I realised that a colleague, who'd already gone down a similar route, had been spot-on.

'Better than therapy,' he'd advised. 'You realise when you go there that it wasn't that bad, after all.'

Technically, I'm not a baby boomer; I miss out by a matter

of months. But I've always aligned myself with the good fortune of the post-war generation, the kids that grew up to reap the benefit of all those social changes: the full employment, the sexual revolution, the travel, the affluence of the eighties and beyond. When I think long and hard about it, we did, mostly, have it all. It might have started badly. And things may look uncertain right now, especially as the baby boomers are 'getting on' in years, not to mention feeling concern for the future of succeeding generations. But luck was on our side. Baby boomers are the historically privileged.

Yet in our nostalgic view of the past, there's a temptation to believe it was all so much safer, more innocent, a much kinder world then. It was, but only in some ways. Our relationships with each other were quite different. In many post-war families, relationships suffered badly, partly because of the consequences of war itself but also because people's lives were stifled, held back by convention, lack of communication – and lack of economic freedom as far as many women were concerned. The bad moments, the personal tragedies, the human failings or weaknesses tended to be unacknowledged, hidden, rarely discussed openly. Authority itself was rarely questioned too. You just got on with it.

Today we are so much richer in our awareness of what makes us and others tick. We can ask lots of questions. And we expect good answers. We take for granted the fact that we can, if we wish, engage in open discourse with others about virtually any topic under the sun. You can argue the toss about which way is better. And there are times when that open, frank exchange does go too far: too much information. But I'm firmly on the side of the present passion for disclosure. When it comes to emotional intelligence, we've come a long way from those bomb-scarred years.

Finally, writing this memoir has made me understand something quite fundamental: my mum's optimistic smile was not merely symbolic of the moment, or even her 'live for now' nature. That bright optimism was a beacon, a guide, not just for me but for everyone. The future, as always, will take care of itself. But what are we as individuals if we cannot look ahead and hope?

Jacky Hyams
London, January 2011

CHAPTER 1
THE VICAR'S BABY

December 22, 1944

Molly could just about manage to move her feet across the sheet until she came across what she'd been hoping for: a hot-water bottle. But the stone bed-warmer was cold now. They'd given her scratchy woollen socks to wear; yet her feet were still freezing. The nurse, the one who'd been quite nice to her until the unbearable pain really started to kick in, was nowhere to be seen. Somewhere in the background, Molly could hear the sounds of babies crying. And despite the big fire still burning in the grate at the far end of the enormous room with its tall windows and high ceilings – had it been a ballroom at some point in its history? she had wondered vaguely when she arrived – all Molly could think now was, 'It's so cold in here. How can they let us lie here freezing like this?'

'Get your sister to bring you a blanket,' came a voice from the next bed. Molly couldn't remember the girl's name, though they'd been quite chatty in the morning, just before Molly actually went into labour. 'She can't come…my mum's

1

really bad,' was all Molly could manage; and only then, once she'd spoken the words, did it all start to sink in: the rushed farewell, hugging her frail and emaciated mum, Bella, back in the Leeds house they'd been evacuated to; the lonely taxi ride in the blackout along the narrow meandering road to the outskirts of Tadcaster until they finally reached the maternity home, a 700-year-old castle with ancient grey stone walls. The castle had been requisitioned by the Ministry of Health to be used as a safe haven for expectant mums when World War II broke out.

Then the last twenty-four hours came rushing back: the increasingly scary labour pains that took over her whole being without warning, until there was nothing else in the world but Molly screaming and shouting, hearing nothing but 'push, push, push, mum' for what seemed like forever until, finally, the words she'd always secretly known she'd hear one day, 'You've got a little girl, Mrs Hyams, a lovely little girl...'

It was all over. She had her little girl! Ginger, of course, wanted a boy, someone to teach football and take to the pub. 'I want us to call him Jack, after Dad,' he'd written confidently from India in his last letter. 'Well, it'll have to be Jacqueline,' thought Molly, struggling to ignore her frozen feet and the soreness and pain all over her body. 'Thank God, there'll be no going down the pub with Ginger and Jack.'

All of a sudden, a flurry of activity on the ward. Three nurses march in across the vast expanse of wooden floor, holding the tightly wrapped newborns for their mothers. It had been busy here last night, three babies born within hours of each other. A starched, trim figure stops at Molly's bed, a nurse she's never seen before, holding the tiny, precious bundle aloft. 'Here you are, Mrs Hyams. Come on, sit up and say hello to your baby,' a voice says briskly.

Slowly, Molly manages to ease herself up. The soreness is awful. But the desire to hold her longed for little girl close for the first time is more powerful. Reaching out, still shaky, she just about manages to get the tiny bundle into her arms. And the exhausted new mum looks down lovingly for the first time into the screwed up, tiny red face of the sleeping infant…

'THAT'S NOT MY BABY!' screams Molly.

'YOU'VE GIVEN ME SOMEONE ELSE'S BABY!'

At first, the nurse won't have any of it. The new mums are not always easy. Hardly surprising with most of the men God knows where and the war still going on. But these women are lucky to go through the ordeal of childbirth in a maternity ward with doctors around – other women have no choice: childbirth frequently happens at home, with help from a local midwife.

'Mrs Hyams.' she soothes. 'This IS your baby.'

But, just to reassure herself, she checks the tiny tag on the baby's foot. Then, without another word, she snatches the tiny bundle from the distraught Molly's arms, and rushes off with it down the length of the vast, chilly room.

Minutes later, she is back at my mother's bedside with the bundle, accompanied by the stern figure of Matron.

'Sorry, Mrs Hyams, it seems there was a bit of a mistake,' explains Matron, dryly, not quite managing to conceal her anger at the mix-up. There will definitely be hell to pay behind the scenes later on.

'Look, Mrs Hyams, here's your little girl now…,' she coos as a relieved, bewildered but nonetheless delighted Molly finally gets to see and cuddle me for the very first time.

Later on, Molly found out what had really happened from the woman in the next bed. A new nurse had been taken on not long before I was born that day in late December. Somehow, in a fit of nerves or sheer panic, she'd mixed up the newborn baby tags. I had been labelled with the surname of the local vicar, and Baby Vicar, in turn, had been labelled 'Hyams'. The vicar's child was a boy, so the mistake would surely have been spotted even without my mother's instinctive reaction. Had the vicar's child been a girl, however, it's quite possible that Molly would have innocently gone back to Leeds with the wrong baby.

And so I came into the world as a near miss, almost a vicar's child by a hair's breadth. A mistake by a nervous young girl could have led to a very different fate, growing up in a chilly northern parsonage, my early life ruled by the diktat of the Church, rather than an East London Jewish kid growing up in a squalid building abutting a bombsite with doting parents who lived for the moment, without too much thought for the future. Or of God, come to that.

So there it is, my arrival in a medieval castle, cast into a chilly world where chaos and confusion reigned. The castle, so ancient it is mentioned in the *Doomsday Book*, is now an upmarket luxury hotel, reputed to be haunted. And guests have been known to report hearing a baby cry long into the night. Even when there were no babies around at the time…

CHAPTER 2
A TELEGRAM

L ike millions of other families, our lives were mired in chaos and uncertainty in the months just before the war ended. We too had our share of bad news as we struggled through the early months of 1945 in our temporary lodgings in Roxholme Grove, Leeds.

In an upstairs bedroom, my grandmother, Bella, lay dying from breast cancer. Molly, helped by her sisters Sarah and Rita, did her best for their mum, helping wash and get her to the toilet, trying hard to tempt her to eat. Outwardly, they acted as if this was a temporary situation – and that she would gradually recover. But everyone knew in their hearts it was hopeless. A doctor had made it clear they could expect the worst.

'Nothing to be done,' he told them bluntly. 'Just try to make sure she eats and drinks whatever she can.' Back then, there was no option of an NHS hospital bed for a sixty-seven-year-old with a terminal illness; indeed, there was no National

Health Service, no morphine to dull the pain, no Macmillan cancer nurses; just another war-weary family struggling to cope with a world turned upside down.

Tears slowly trickled down Bella's pale, shrunken face the day Molly came home from the castle with her precious bundle. She'd been quite brave up till then, despite the terrible pain. But she broke down when she saw me for the first time.

'I'll never see her grow up,' she sobbed, while my grandfather, Oliver, hovered at her bedside, unsure of his place in a sickroom.

Still fit and dapper in his seventies, Oliver coped with his wife's distress by leaving the room. In fact, he left the house as often as was decently possible. Ignoring the harsh northern winter, smartly dressed in his pinstripe suit and big overcoat, he went out for long walks most days. He had been a good provider for his family of eight children, working long hours as a tailor and cutter to the fine ladies who shopped in the big London department stores in the early 1900s. Even in the thirties, when times became more difficult, he'd managed to keep working. As a husband, however, he fell short: his daughters knew all too well that their parents' marriage had been an unhappy liaison, arranged by their respective Jewish families just months before the pair had fled the Russian pogroms (the anti-Jewish violence that swept across Russia in the late 1800s) to settle in England.

In St Petersburg, Bella, eighteen, had fallen in love with a neighbour, a handsome young Russian boy. But he wasn't Jewish. So her parents had promptly married her off to Oliver, who was.

Already in the late stages of pregnancy when the couple

boarded the boat for the long journey to England, Bella and Oliver's first child, Jane, was born prematurely on the boat – and remained stateless throughout her life. Bella had struggled to adjust to their new life in London as pregnancy had followed pregnancy for the better part of fifteen years. Later in life, she'd confided to her daughters that Oliver's relentless, constant desire for sex, regardless of her own needs or feelings, had made the marriage close to a living hell for her.

Married to a man she couldn't love, worn down by his incessant physical demands, she poured all her love and affection into her offspring, spoiling the four older boys rotten – the traditional Russian way – while leaving the girls to help with all the hard work around the home. Except for Molly, that was, the baby of the family, who was almost as spoilt and indulged as the boys.

Now, with their mother's life ebbing away upstairs, Bella's three youngest daughters sat huddled in front of the fire in the living room of their lodgings in the draughty Leeds house, dreading the worst and apprehensive about the future, while I lay sleeping in my tiny cot in the girls' shared bedroom.

Rita, the oldest of the trio at 32, had already been married twice. Her first somewhat reckless marriage, to a Russian Communist called Georgy, had ended in divorce. Her second husband, Hans, an academic, had died unexpectedly from a brain tumour. Undaunted by her misfortune, she was the most restless and adventurous of the girls.

'I've had a letter from Hans's parents in Kenya,' she told her sisters, in an attempt to break the gloom.

'They want me to go and see them when the war's over,' she confided.

'I've always wanted to see Africa, so this is my big chance.'

'You can't start making plans about something like that now,' snapped Sarah bitterly. 'You mother's dying – or hadn't you noticed?'

Molly peered at her older sister. 'What's got into Sarah?' she wondered. But by the look on Sarah's face, she figured it was best to keep quiet. The outburst was completely out of character. Normally, Sarah was quiet, shy, even withdrawn. She kept herself to herself. Molly couldn't ever remember her sister shouting or snapping like this at anyone.

'You're acting as if the war's going to be over any minute!' Sarah said loudly, her face starting to redden with anger.

'No one's really sure what's going to happen. My friend Vera in London says the Germans are still dropping those horrible V2 bombs all over the place and some people are saying the Allies are stuck in Italy. Why can't you think a bit about what's going on around you, you stupid woman!'

Rita shrugged. Unruffled by Sarah's retort, she dipped into her handbag and took out a powder compact, clicking it open to check her make-up.

'You're right, Sis,' sighed Molly, getting up to go upstairs to peek into my cot, wondering what the hell was wrong with Sarah but anxious to leave the room before things got too heated. 'They keep telling us it'll be over soon but we're all in the dark really. God knows when Ginger will be coming back from India.'

My dad, Ginger, had been serving in the Royal Army Pay Corps, stationed in Foots Cray, near Sidcup in Kent, ever since the call-up, not long before he and my mum had married in the spring of 1940 after a courtship of over four years. They'd met in a youth club in Clapton, East London, where both their families lived at the time. But after his unexpected posting overseas in April 1944, when Molly discovered she was expecting me, she and her family chose to move to the comparative safety of Leeds, rather than continuing to risk facing the chaos of the London bombings.

Not exactly the patriotic type, Ginger had originally toyed with the idea of deserting – 20,000 men who couldn't face the idea of being in the armed forces did just that – but Molly, normally easy-going, had put her foot down when he'd suggested it.

'I'm not going to be a deserter's wife, Ging,' she'd said with typical good sense. 'You can't go on the run like that. It's not fair on me.'

And so my dad reluctantly did his duty. An eye injury as a child meant he wasn't deemed fit for combat so he remained in a Pay Corps clerical desk job in Foots Cray throughout nearly four years of war. He'd been working alongside his father Jack in the family business in the East End just before war broke out. Jack was a commission agent (a polite word for bookmaker) so my dad, technically a commission agent's clerk, was accustomed to a desk job. But the sudden posting overseas with the Pay Corps, destination unknown – until his first letters had started to arrive from faraway India – had been an unexpected separation. They'd hoped to see out the war together in London.

But while Molly shared with millions the all-too-common uncertainty of a loved one thousands of miles away, what no one knew that cold January night was that Sarah was quietly nursing a tragic secret, one she couldn't bring herself to reveal to anyone.

Just a week before, there'd been an unexpected knock at the front door in the early afternoon. Apart from her bedridden mother, no one else was at home. Rita was at the shops and Oliver had gone for one of his long walks; Molly had taken me to briefly visit a friend living in separate lodgings in a nearby street.

Sarah stared at the man on the doorstep. He'd arrived by bike; he looked terribly young. He had a telegram in his gloved hand.

'Are you Mrs Lang?' he said, his voice low, hating his job, the war, the winter.

'Yes I am,' said Sarah, the fear and dread already rising in her, wanting to slam the door shut in the young man's face and run away for ever.

Sarah knew exactly what this meant. You heard about it often enough. Sometimes you dreamed that it was happening to you.

But like the polite, self-contained woman she was, she took the envelope, thanked the man politely, closed the front door and walked slowly into the kitchen to read its contents. At first, she just stared at the words in the telegram. Then she re-read it over again. But she didn't cry. She just heated up some water in the kettle, lit the gas and made herself a cup of tea. Later, she tore the hated piece of paper into a hundred tiny pieces. It would be months before she let herself weep. And then, of course, she couldn't stop.

Sarah was thirty, with a career in the Civil Service. The very opposite of my mum who was pretty, lively and flirtatious, Sarah was studious, serious and quite prim; by then, no one had really expected her to marry. Yet until the telegram arrived, she'd been a married woman for six months. She had met Anton, an Austrian Jewish refugee who'd enlisted in the Pioneer Corps, at a dance in London. In typical wartime fashion, there'd been a rushed courtship and a proposal just before he was due to be posted overseas.

'But what if you don't come back?' asked Sarah when they discussed it all.

'Don't worry, I'll come back,' he said confidently. 'The war will be over soon, anyway.'

After their register office wedding, Anton was posted overseas, somewhere in Europe. They'd managed just one weekend together in London as man and wife. Now he was dead. Killed by a devastating V2 rocket attack on a packed Antwerp cinema, while on brief leave visiting his brother in Belgium. 567 people died in that attack on the Rex in Antwerp, the highest single death toll from one rocket attack during the war in Europe. It happened just four days before I was born in the castle.

Sarah kept her sad secret through that miserable Leeds winter of 1945. Only after Bella's funeral in April, weeks before VE Day in May signalled the official end of the war, did she blurt out the truth to her family.

'I just couldn't bring myself to talk about it what with mum lying there in such pain and you with the baby,' she told Molly.

Shocked, Molly had comforted her widowed sister as best she could. At that point, it looked like tears and sorrow had virtually engulfed their life. Nursing Bella through her last few weeks of pain and anguish, helpless at watching a loved one suffer, would haunt the sisters for many years to come.

Yet somehow, like the rest of the country exhausted by the daily struggle of wartime existence, they had no option other than to put their feelings aside and get on with the business of living.

With his wife gone, Oliver wanted to remain in Leeds, as did their older sister Jane. 'I'm too old to start again in London and Jane will be here,' he told his family.

And so the family started to splinter: Rita did go to Africa in 1946; she never lived in England again. Sarah too would eventually strike out for the unknown in Canada after the war, never to return.

With her other siblings scattered – two brothers still posted overseas, the other two married with young families, far away from London – Molly had to make her own plans for us. And sure enough, days after their mother's funeral, a letter arrived from her father-in-law, Jack, known as The Old Man by his family, in London's East End.

'I've managed to find a flat in Hackney, off the Kingsland Road near Dalston, for you and the baby,' he wrote. 'The rent's one pound a week. It's only temporary but it means you'll have a roof over your head for when Ginger comes home. I've paid the key money, so you don't have to worry.'

Molly could only feel grateful and hugely relieved. Finding a habitable flat to rent anywhere in London was a monumental and daunting task, with so many bombed-out ruined buildings everywhere and some homeless families with no option other than to live temporarily in rest centres, temporary shelters set up by the authorities (often in school buildings) to house those whose homes had become uninhabitable due to enemy action and who could not make any alternative housing arrangements.

And, even if you were prepared to get up at dawn to stand in a queue of hundreds if you managed to spot a flat up for rent, you still needed hard cash to hand over to greedy private landlords: a bit of a problem for Molly with her tiny soldier's wife's allowance.

Ginger's mum and dad, poles apart from her own more cultured, Russian-born parents, were Jewish cockneys from Petticoat Lane, with a fierce attachment to their patch of London; they'd toughed it out in the very heart of the devastated city, blithely ignoring the Blitz, the bomb craters, the blackouts and the wrecked buildings around them.

Now, in typically resourceful fashion, they'd given their eldest son's wife a helping hand just when it was needed most. Molly hadn't even asked for help – The Old Man just did it. Though Dalston, with its shabby East London surrounds and badly bomb-damaged houses with rubble everywhere, wasn't exactly Molly's first choice as a place to raise a family; she'd grown up in the slightly more respectable confines of West London.

'Oh well, whatever the flat's like, it'll be a start for us,' mused Molly, picking me up to cuddle me for the umpteenth time. 'It's just temporary, anyway.'

A few weeks later, my mum, Sarah and I boarded the packed train from Leeds back to London, joining the melee of other families, evacuees and soldiers heading back to the capital. Trains were so slow and infrequent then you had to get to the station several hours before the departure time just to make sure you'd actually get on. And the journey took nearly 10 hours.

But the long hours on the train didn't seem to matter to the two dark-haired slender women who eventually struggled out of the carriage with their heavy cases and a tiny baby onto the crowded platform at King's Cross Station.

Peacetime lay ahead. What could be better than that?

CHAPTER 3
A HOMECOMING

We are on a crowded trolley bus, seated near the door, en route to Ridley Road market. It's only a few stops but today, Molly doesn't fancy carrying me, less than two years old, all the way down the narrow reaches of the Kingsland Road and back, especially with a shopping bag.

At the first stop, a tall, thin man jumps on. He's in uniform, maybe newly demobbed. He plonks himself down on the seat opposite us. I peer at him with considerable childish curiousness. Then, as recognition dawns, I start waving a chubby fist in his face.

'Daddy, Daddy!' I yell at the top of my voice.

'Is my Daddy!'

Heads turn. A few people get what's happening and start to smile. Someone even titters. So many children with dads they've never met only know him as a photo, a man dressed in Forces uniform. But Molly is awash with embarrassment.

'Ssh,' she warns me. 'It's not your daddy, Daddy's in India.'

I ignore this. 'Daddy!' I squeal, reaching out my little arms to the uniformed man, eager to establish a connection.

For months, a black-and-white photo of Ginger, proudly posing in his Pay Corps uniform, has stood on the mantelpiece. On the back, my dad's scrawled inscription: 'To my darling wife and baby daughter, with all my love and devotion, Ging'. It was one of several photos he'd posted from Meerut, India, the administrative centre where the Pay Corps were based.

Now the man is smiling. He's admiring my mum, her Victory Roll hair, bright red lipstick, earrings, smart tailored suit, slim ankles and siren's slingbacks. She's a dish, my mum, a petite glamour girl lighting up the post-war gloom. All around us, harassed women duck down the Kingsland Road in scarves, curlers and drab, shapeless utility gear. But not Molly. Even without my little outburst, she'd be turning male heads today.

'Wouldn't mind being your daddy,' the man mutters, at which point the bus jerks to a stop. Molly pretends not to have heard him, scoops me up in her arms and we're off the bus and on the pavement.

'Daddy's in India,' she tells me again.

And to herself she sighs, 'And it's about time they let him come home.'

By now, we've more or less settled into the flat that The Old Man found for us in a three-storey brick block with a curious turret shape, in a tiny, narrow street, practically an alleyway, just off Shacklewell Lane, a winding road that meanders down towards Hackney Downs.

Molly hadn't exactly been overwhelmed with joy the day she

saw our new home. The block, in the middle of the narrow street, had bombed-out houses each side. One house on the corner of Shacklewell Lane was badly damaged but seemed to be inhabited still; Molly spotted a pale-faced boy peering at her from a window. There was some kind of wrecked yard directly opposite the block of flats. Everywhere you looked, there was rubble and damage.

Before the war, this part of London had been very much a rundown industrial area; clothing factories abounded in Shacklewell Lane and around Kingsland Road. Now it was like so much of East London: a shattered, wrecked wasteland. A few factories had survived and were running, though. Somehow, people continued to live, work and love amidst this chaos. Molly was as familiar with the landscape of wartime havoc as any other Londoner who'd remained there for most of the war; she'd worked as an underwear saleslady in Jax, in Oxford Street, only to turn up for work one morning to find the shop a smouldering ruin. And even in Leeds, which had suffered comparatively few air raids, bomb damage was still evident.

Yet this place, for some reason, seemed especially desolate. And the second-floor flat, with its narrow hallway and small, dingy rooms, seemed so pokey after all the rented flats in the big high-ceilinged Victorian houses she'd grown up in. The flat was damp too; Hackney, built on marshland, was always one of London's dampest boroughs.

'I know I should be grateful, Sis,' Molly told Sarah after we'd moved in.

'Without The Old Man, we'd have been stuck. People are queuing up everywhere to rent places much worse than this – and paying over the odds for it.

'But it's so...depressing. I want the baby to grow up somewhere nicer. But we'll just have to be patient, I s'pose.'

Sarah thought Molly had a raw deal, though she didn't say so. She stayed with us frequently in the flat, helping my mum with me and generally making herself useful until getting a post in Berlin, to work with the Control Commission.

Though we'd moved in with just a few suitcases, in time a few sticks of furniture were acquired, mostly with the help of The Old Man, who had useful contacts everywhere.

Furniture, like many things, was rationed. So, like the bombed out or evacuated masses, we made do with the bare minimum, mostly second-hand: a rickety wardrobe, an ancient gas cooker, some crockery, linens, mostly sourced from nearby market stalls, a few ornaments the sisters had managed to pack up and bring from Leeds.

My little cot was in the corner of the main bedroom where my mum slept. When with us, Sarah slept in the tiny damp second bedroom facing the street – the space that eventually became my room.

Heating in the flat came from small coal fires, tiny grates in thirties-tiled fireplaces in the living room and the main bedroom. The flat had a bathroom with a bath, toilet and sink. But constant hot running water was an undreamed of luxury. All hot water was boiled on the gas stove. (Our Ascot water heater didn't arrive until quite a few years later.) The pocket-sized kitchen boasted very little, no fridge, microwave, washing machine or dishwasher; these were, of course, light years away. The main household appliance, apart from a kettle, was the mangle, the contraption you had to have to wring out the washing and get it to a semi-dry state.

Basically, the kitchen was just a sink with cold running water, the gas cooker and a pantry with several shelves for storage of crockery and food. Had you peered inside our pantry in those days you'd have found gold-coloured tins of powdered eggs from the US and sickly sweet orange juice bottles amid the meagre assortment of vegetables, mostly potatoes, which weren't rationed but were still hard to find sometimes, and carrots, which were also not rationed and were plentiful (people believed that eating carrots helped you see better in the blackout years); plus small amounts of butter and cheese, carefully wrapped up in crumpled greaseproof paper.

I bonded with Sarah in those early months; for a while she and my mum formed my entire world. One day, without warning, at just over a year old, I stood up in the little cot and opened my mouth.

'Sis,' I ventured, my mum's nickname for Sarah, much to the sisters' delight. It wasn't long before I was proudly informing passers-by, 'I'm 18 months.' BBC radio, of course, was an early educational and musical influence: along with 26 million others, we tuned in to the Light Programme record request show *Two-Way Family Favourites* each Sunday at midday; the signature tune 'With a Song in My Heart' was the prelude to the traditional Sunday roast across the country throughout the late forties and fifties. My first ever attempt at recitation came after I struggled to mimic the announcer reading out the Shipping Forecast: 'Cromarty, Forth, Tyne, Dogger' – faraway places that were meaningless to us. Yet the sounds, heard day after day, week in, week out, meant the words were processed, fixed firmly in my memory.

Money was tight. My mum's sole income as a soldier's wife with a child was a small allowance, so we were heavily subsidised by my dad's parents. Each Friday, they'd organise a major food delivery – carrier bags from Petticoat Lane delivered to our front door by one of her father-in-law's army of 'runners' from the 'Lane' as we called it, men who worked as casual delivery men, mostly for The Old Man's betting business, usually collecting cash or betting slips from punters in pubs and on street corners. Inside the carrier bags were all manner of foodstuffs mostly off the ration books via the 'black market': fish and meat, eggs, butter (the ration of two ounces didn't go very far) and any delicacies they could procure along the way like tinned peaches or salmon.

Molly wasn't a big eater so the combination of what was officially available to us on the ration books plus the extra black-market goodies from the Lane meant we were well fed, at least.

As a toddler, I was crazy for anything sweet, an inheritance of my mother's own love of sweets and sugar. (Late in life she confessed that she'd eaten mainly 'nosh', or sweets, throughout her pregnancy.) Chocolate spread was my particular favourite, 'bread and bread and chocolate spread' an early mantra. Since both bread and sugar remained on ration long after the war ended (bread until 1948 and sweets until 1953), my endless cravings for sugar were sometimes satisfied via the black-market goodies that arrived in those weekly deliveries. But even so, a whole block of chocolate or a proper box of chocolates was virtually unknown. You didn't ever see such things.

And so it turned out that when my father finally did get his demob papers and came home to us in the flat, his arrival from overseas and into our lives was somewhat overshadowed – by a big box of Cadbury's.

It's spring and I am wearing a little white dress with smocking, sent to us by my mother's sister, Rita, who knitted and sewed beautifully and supplied my mum with regular clothing items for me before she left for Africa.

The front door to our flat is open and a strange man walks in, flinging his bags down in the narrow hallway.

I run, curly-haired and chubby-legged, down the hallway towards the man. I know who it is, because I've been primed in advance.

'Is my daddy!' I shout, my claim to the man who until now had lived on the mantelpiece.

My dad, thin and pale from bouts of malaria, his civvies virtually hanging off him after his epic sea journey from India, throws his bags on the floor and scoops me up for a welcoming hug, the baby he's seen in pictures, already a chatterbox toddler. He's got a present for me. 'Wait till you see what I've got for you,' he chuckles. Then he lugs the bags into the bedroom and emerges, minutes later, beaming all over and sporting his Big Homecoming Gift.

For a first effort, it was outstanding. Never in the history of post-war gift giving has a small child been so thrilled, so enraptured by a homecoming offering.

Looking back, it was magnificent booty for the times. How did he manage to obtain this astonishing gift? Even now, in my mind's eye, I see it as an enormous box. And inside the prized purple square box are what seem, to me, to be hundreds of Cadbury's chocolates, delights of all shapes and sizes – square ones, thin ones, hard toffee, oozy caramel, orange flavoured, ginger, soft and hard centres, chocolate after chocolate after chocolate. A sugary bonanza. I'm squirming, squealing with delight.

My parents, together at last, carelessly let me take ownership of the box. Perhaps if they hadn't been so distracted by the occasion – it had been over two years since they clapped eyes on each other – they might have thought to take the box away from me and hide it somewhere safe, away from prying little hands. But this is their reunion, their big day. It's a lot to cope with, seeing each other again and meeting a toddler you've only known through photos.

So that's how the chocolates became mine and mine alone. I was destined to be a spoilt only child, indulged by parents who adored me and never really knew how to say no. And the indulgence all started the day Ginger came home from the war with that big box of chocolates. Because once I have the sweets to myself, there's no stopping me. Greedy isn't the word. I determinedly chomp my way, choccy after choccy, through the lot. Like most greedy guts, the more I eat, the less I taste or savour. I just cram them into my tiny gob, one after the other, an orgy of sugar. Until there are no more chocolates left nestling alluringly in their little dark-brown paper homes. And my pretty white dress is ruined with stains, an early sign of the slobbery that never quite left me.

'Oh God, Ging, she's eaten the lot!' moans Molly.

'Aah, don't worry Mol, I knew she'd love 'em,' says my dad, who at thirty four knows a lot about doing arithmetic and placing bets on 'geegees', but has much to learn about raising kids.

But the reality is, of course, I have eaten far too many in one go. And the consequences of this are dramatic, if somewhat delayed.

For the very next morning, as the returned soldier lies sleeping, my mum decides to pop out with me to the newsagents in Shacklewell Lane. 'We'll go get daddy a paper,' she tells me.

But on the way back, just as we reach our block of flats, I start to wail. To put it in the simplest terms, my body decides to shed itself of the unaccustomed load. Right there. All over the pavement.

Up the stone stairs Molly drags me, screaming like a banshee, a hideous yellow trail of smelly poo in our wake. Not only have I managed to shame us publicly on the first morning of my dad's return, the evidence is there for the delectation of our neighbours.

'Now I'll have to go down there and clean it up,' Molly fumes, before marching me into the bathroom to hurriedly clean and change me.

And later, as she kneels on the stairs with brush and pail, furiously scrubbing the evidence of my greed away, sure enough, our most detested neighbour, Maisie the ground-floor shrew, stands there and takes a pop.

'Gotta bit of a tummy problem your little Jacky, eh Mrs Hyams?' she lobs at my mum.

My mum doesn't answer, just carries on scrubbing, seething inwardly. It's a nasty, if somewhat unhygienic, task, removing the evidence of your daughter's greed, there for all to see. And she feels slightly guilty for not realising beforehand the implications of indulging my chocolate frenzy.

'Shame, really. And your 'usband just back 'ome, is 'e?' continues Maisie, determined to exploit every second of our shame, already planning to circulate the latest morsel of gossip about that snooty woman and her little curly-haired brat.

Right from day one, we'd stuck out like sore thumbs in the confined, narrow street – far too well dressed, too many overflowing carrier bags coming to our door – and this is a triumphant moment for her. In fact, it's the defining moment in our relationship for the years ahead.

'Yeah, Ginger's back now,' says Molly grimly, longing to throw the contents of the smelly bucket right in her neighbour's face but just about managing to contain herself.

'We'll probably be moving soon,' she says, half to herself, half to her loathsome neighbour.

'Hah! You'll be lucky!' spits Maisie as a parting shot before retreating to the murky interior of her ground floor cave.

They never spoke again, not once in the decades that followed. Maisie's son, Alf, a scrawny scruff around my age, was pointedly ignored by us too if we encountered them on the stairs. I never had a conversation with him, nor did I want to; he was a bit too smelly, too much of a ruffian, for comfort.

Yet Maisie was a bit of a witch in some ways. Her prediction was eerily accurate.

There never was a move from the damp flat for my mother, not until forty-four years later when the removal van arrived to help move her to a better, warmer flat in a nearby security building.

And while other post-war kids might remember the day their unknown soldier dad came home with delight or bewilderment – the divorce rate in England and Wales soared once the demob was over, from 12,314 in 1944 to 60,190 in 1947 – my memories are only of a strange, skinny man with an enormous box of chocolates. And a vivid lesson in the nasty consequences of overindulgence.

CHAPTER 4
BETS ARE ON

My dad was one of the later returnees to civilian life post World War II. Five million men and women had served in the British Armed Forces. The somewhat slow, frustrating process of 'bringing the boys home' started mid-1945, but it wasn't until early 1947 that the demob finally ended. Exhausted, broke and surrounded by the debris of nearly six years of war, what were my dad's career prospects?

A knockabout East-End roisterer who'd only opted to settle down when war broke out – 'Ginger and I got married because everyone else was doing it' – was my mum's somewhat romantic take on their courtship, which had started in the late thirties and had been, for much of the time, an on-off situation.

A steady bloke he wasn't. The younger Ginger often worked 'on the knocker', selling goods door to door all over south-east England, so he was frequently away. He'd only reluctantly joined his dad in the betting business just before war broke out, preferring the freedom of the road to any real commitment.

Yet as they courted in the late thirties, he became fiercely attached to my mum, who was five years his junior; petite, dark, slim and fashionably turned out, she was a bit of a man magnet. And her cheerful, easy-going manner was equally attractive. As their relationship developed, my dad had a somewhat disturbing habit of sending one or two close friends to my mum's house to 'keep an eye on Molly' when his knockabout life meant he'd be unavailable. Even during the war, when they'd started married life in a bedsit in Finsbury Park in London, his posting to Kent meant they weren't together very much. On leave, he'd head for the pub most nights. So in a way, he'd led a semi-bachelor existence for years, his passions typical of the times: boxing, soccer, pubs, and lots of laughs. Even in Meerut, he'd managed to indulge himself with visits to the races, placing bets and playing soccer. (He sent us many photos to prove it.)

Now here he was in his mid-thirties, living full-time with a wife and a small child. One hundred per cent responsibility, which I suspect gave him the willies.

Though he'd left school at fourteen and was poorly educated, my dad had a head for figures and a talent for words – his letters home to my mum from India were beautifully written – so he could, at a push, have found steady work in a clerical position in an office after the war. He'd got brownie points from his superiors in the Pay Corps. 'The Army always wanted Ging,' my mum would frequently tell me as I grew up, her badge of pride that his destiny as a street bookie could easily have been otherwise.

But, of course, as a typical East Ender who'd grown up in Petticoat Lane around long-term duckers and divers with varying degrees of commercial success, the disciplined confines of army life, regular if low pay, and with some sort of permanence ahead, had scant appeal for my dad. And he needed cash. Fast. There was a wife and kid to consider now. So he took up the first offer that came his way – to work alongside his dad in Jack's betting business.

The betting laws of the time were draconian: technically, it was only legal to place a bet if you were at the racecourse or the dog track. Well-heeled punters could legally run an account and have credit with a 'commission agent' working out of an office – but the commission agent was only permitted to take bets by phone. Out on the street or in the pub, handing over cash to place bets on dogs or horses was technically illegal, right up until the early sixties.

But there was a great deal of money to be made illegally because back then, betting on 'the geegees', or horses (and, to a lesser extent, the dogs) was more or less a national pastime. Gambling a few bob from their weekly pay was the working man's one and only chance to improve his lot. The football pools had also started by then – but the daily or weekly bet was incredibly popular everywhere, just like the Lottery is nowadays.

This national passion for the odd bet meant that Ginger and The Old Man were in a prime position to exploit the post-war hunger for illegal betting. For a start, they were in a very good spot, in the heart of bustling, busy Petticoat Lane, renamed Middlesex Street in 1830 (by the Victorians who wanted to avoid references to women's underwear), though everyone continued to call it by its original name. Their little 'commission agent' shop on Middlesex Street was very close to

Houndsditch in the City of London precinct, the junction where the time-honoured East-End hustlers or traders and the more respectable City gents, or 'bowler hats', merged. Consequently, the law wasn't much of a problem: a friendly bobby from the local constabulary would usually turn a blind eye to cash being handed over for bets in the pubs and streets nearby: a well placed 'bung', or cash bribe, usually also handed over in the pub, saw to that little fly in the ointment. And while it was all fairly new to my dad, The Old Man knew the terrain well; he'd been running a family business in the Lane for most of his life.

Before the betting business had been launched, the Middlesex Street premises had been a coal shop: this, in turn, had morphed over time from a local horse-drawn delivery business, though Jack's dad, my great grandfather, had gone bankrupt more than once. So the network of contacts, both legal and otherwise, that Jack had made through a lifetime there meant my dad had a Chief Fixer to back him up if there were any problems. And as a Fixer, The Old Man certainly carried a bit of clout in the area.

One day, not long after my dad came home, one of the newer runners that Jack had employed to take bets and pay punters was picked up by the police. A lone copper spotted him carrying an unusually large bundle down Middlesex Street and, as suspected, further investigation revealed it contained some black-market 'gear', in this case, several dozen pairs of trousers, all new, sourced from who knows where. Clothing, of course, was still rationed then. This was definitely a 'sus' package, a discovery that could lead to a court appearance and a hefty fine.

Yet when the copper, also new to the area, marched the handcuffed and nervous man into the police station, his sergeant looked up in surprise.

'He works for Jack Hyams, you fool. Get him outta here – or there'll be trouble!'

So there it was. Jack wasn't exactly a mafioso making people offers they couldn't refuse but my grandfather was well established in his 'manor'. So I doubt my dad agonised over his career choice. And my mum wouldn't have tried to dissuade him, anyway. She was happy. Ging was back, she knew he wouldn't see her short and, joy of joys, she had her little girl to look after. Yet she was determined to stick with an only child. A boy, instinct told her, would be A Bad Thing.

'I'm definitely not having any more,' she wrote in a letter to Sarah, who'd decided to emigrate to Canada after her time in Germany.

'I always wanted a little girl and I got a little girl. A boy would wind up drinking in the pub all the time, just like Ginger and The Old Man.'

Such single-mindedness was in contrast to my mum's easy-going demeanour. Maybe she was already concerned about our less-than-salubrious environment. Two kids in the tiny flat would have been a nightmare – it was bad enough humping a pushchair up and down the stone stairs when I was very little – though many still lived in far worse conditions, of course. But essentially, Ginger and Molly, hugely relieved that the war was finally over, just wanted to get on with life. They didn't have ambition in the sense we now understand it. It was enough for them that they'd come through it all. The future would take care of itself. And my dad's cash income as an illegal bookie would see us right.

And so began a routine, six days a week, that remained fairly unwavering for nearly two decades: each morning, my dad, smartly suited and booted, would take the number 649 bus down the Kingsland Road to Liverpool Street and make his way to the Lane and the 'commission agent' office, to take bets from the more affluent punters who had a phone, could ring through their bets and run an account: all totally legit. Early evening – and at lunchtime – once the pubs were open, he'd stroll round the corner to Houndsditch and park himself at the bar of the George & Dragon, drinking, wisecracking, swapping stories or taking illegal bets from punters; his usual gang of cronies, small-time crooks, market stallholders and cops around him, ordering big rounds of drinks for all and generally having a whale of a time. The Old Man, now in his sixties, would sometimes join him. But he was slowing down somewhat, hence his need for his son and heir to step in and keep the punters happy.

The pub doubled as a virtual office. If Ginger had a good day's wins and came out ahead, the rounds for his gang – and often anyone else who happened to drop in – were frequent and generous. If he'd lost, the rounds were a bit more muted. Then, usually at closing time, he'd hail a cab by Liverpool Street station to take him down the sometimes foggy, almost traffic-free, streets to Dalston and home. On Sundays, when there was no racing, he'd usually venture out to the pub for the 12 to 2pm session, come home, eat lunch and sleep off the week's transactions.

This was his working life, primarily a man's world and a pretty macho one at that.

The first time he took my mum into a pub and asked her what she wanted to drink, she timorously suggested an orange squash.

My dad looked at her and started laughing.

'An orange squash!'

'Umm…well, I think that would be nice…or a lemonade,' said my poor mum, floundering, not really knowing what she should be asking for since it was the first time she'd even been inside a public house. Public houses, East End or otherwise, did not form any part of the world she'd grown up in. They were totally unknown territory.

'Look, I can't go up to the bar and ask for lemonade,' explained my dad patiently to this attractive young woman he'd already fallen for. She always seemed to be smiling. Or laughing.

'They all know me in here. They'll think there's something wrong with me if I do that. 'ave a gin and it (gin with Italian vermouth), instead.'

That, in a nutshell, was my dad's world. Buying stiff drinks, taking bets, having a laugh, taking the mickey out of his cronies – my dad was a terrible prankster, often crudely humorous. The butt of his jokes would often be the neighbours in the Lane and their families. One example was a Polish family who lived around the corner from the office. At some point, the family, whose surname was unpronounceable to locals, had been dubbed 'The Polos'. Over time, as the mother produced child after child, one each year until there were seven kids, the nickname changed to reflect the popular advert of the late fifties: Polo, the mint with a hole.

Then, somehow, Mrs Polo became known around the place as 'the bint wiv an 'ole'.

Having the bookies' wad of readies to flash around obviously gave my dad a bit of gravitas in the upside-down, post-war East-End world, where one section of the population had very little and really struggled to get by, while the others, the traders, black marketeers or stallholders with cash, traded back and forth in virtually anything portable that you can think of – and didn't really go without much. Unless, of course, they had a serious betting habit – and many did.

Even in those cash-poor years, it wasn't unknown for the occasional dedicated punter to lay down a 'monkey' (£500) on a single bet. When you consider that even a 'pony' (£25) represented roughly two-and-a-half times the average working man's weekly wages in the late forties, it's obvious that some bookies were scoring very high in the prosperity stakes. And quite a few gambling men lost their shirts – and more.

All in all, accepting illegal bets probably seemed like a soft option when you take into account what so many in the country had endured through the blackouts, the bombs, the devastated lives and epic shortages of wartime – and still continued to struggle with in the years that followed. Is it any wonder that Ginger decided to take the easy option, throw the dice – and hope for the best?

CHAPTER 5

NEIGHBOURS

Our street wasn't exactly the sort of place you'd wistfully recall as the setting for an idyllic, rose-tinted childhood reverie. No gardens, fields or open spaces. You'd hear the odd sparrow chirping sometimes, but that was the only evidence of nature around us. This place was narrow and bleak, scarred by war damage and years of poverty. In the thirties, the area had been part of the beginnings of slum clearance. But then war broke out. Socially, the street also defied the somewhat sentimental legend that the chirpy, chippy East Enders endured the worst of the war years and beyond by sticking together like glue, helping each other out frequently and popping in and out of each other's homes all the time.

Perhaps this was true elsewhere. But it didn't apply here; the daily struggle to survive, feed the family and keep going took up all of our neighbours' energy. People would greet each other, chat briefly – 'looks like it's gonna rain' – then go about their business. There were fewer invitations to come round for a cuppa and cheerful, friendly exchanges than my mum had known in Leeds, where locals had made the evacuated family welcome. In any case, apart from our block of 12 flats, built in the late thirties but having mysteriously survived the bombs and the chaos, there weren't any neat rows of terrace houses to pop in and out of. If you're living amid ruin, relying on meagre rations to feed yourself and your family, you're unlikely to be inviting the people next door round for a slap-up meal.

The tiny street was dominated by the handiwork of the Luftwaffe. Adjacent to our block of flats were the bombed-out remnants of what had once been two modest workmen's cottages. Inside one of these derelict ruins, living heaven knows how, was a 'foreign' couple, rumoured to be from a faraway place called Cyprus. They never talked to anyone. And adjacent to the bombed-out cottages was what had once been a third one, knocked down by the local authority just before the war as part of the planned slum clearance and then turned into a public bomb shelter.

Almost opposite the old shelter was the front door to the corner house, badly wrecked but still inhabited by the Coopers, their toddler kids Bobby and his sister Mary, the family waiting stoically, like so many others, for the authorities to rehouse them. Their home, though damaged, damp and dark, was technically deemed to be 'habitable', so they had to wait a few years. Not surprisingly, all conversations with Mrs Cooper tended to be dominated by this topic.

'I've 'eard nuffink from those bleeding bastards down the 'ousing department Mrs 'yams,' was Mrs Cooper's perennial greeting.

''Ow do they fink we can bring up two kids in a piss 'ole like this?'

She had a point. The Coopers had an outside loo but no bathroom; they'd have to go to Hackney Baths once a week, if that, if they wanted a bath, rather than a strip wash. The third bombsite, at the other end of our street, had also been a family house. When we moved into the area it was nothing more than bricks, dust, debris and rubbish; indeed, it gradually became a bit of a playground for local roughnecks, until the authorities constructed a tin wall around it, too high for even the most determined street chancer to clamber over.

Over time, this site became a sort of tumbledown car yard, run by an older man called Charlie and his son, Len. It was never really clear what they actually did inside the yard – or how they'd come to acquire the site from the authorities – but from time to time, as I grew up, you'd see them tinkering with various kinds of vehicles in the yard, sometimes at night.

Len and Charlie were unfailingly polite to my mum when she passed, always greeting her cheerfully, sometimes even offering to help her if she had heavy shopping. But there were no proper conversations. In a way, their attitude to us was more like a bit of forelock tugging, respect for your betters, than normal everyday neighbourliness. We stood out like sore thumbs in our milieu: smartly dressed, well fed, living a well-shod life in these squalid surroundings.

As for the other flat dwellers, we mostly just glimpsed them in passing. Families came and went in some of the other dwellings without us ever exchanging more than the odd hello. Apart from Maisie and Alf in the centre ground-floor flat, that is, who were pointedly ignored by us after the

Chocolates Incident. They'd drawn a bit of a short straw when they moved in: their front entrance was directly behind the entry door for all the rubbish that poured down from all floors via The Chute.

Everyone in the block had one thing in common: we detested everything about The Chute, an unsanitary and unsavoury repository for the block's rubbish. Each floor had access to a wall-mounted square metal opening to The Chute; you climbed up or down one flight of stairs to get to it. Yet the opening itself was badly designed and far too narrow for the amount of rubbish that got chucked down it. As a result, The Chute was frequently blocked. To compound matters, rubbish collection from the tip that piled up behind the ground floor door was pretty unreliable. So in summer you frequently held your nose as you clambered up the stone stairs as a couple of weeks' worth of rubbish lay festering behind the door. The block stank to high heaven – and buzzed with flies.

In the flat directly above us lived Mary, a blind woman in her late fifties, alone and cut off from the world. Relatives would shop for her and bring the necessities to her door or give her a hand once a week. And about once a year, someone would collect Mary, help her down the six steep flights of stone stairs, and take her out for the day. The rest of the time she lived there, frustrated with her lot – who can blame her? – but venting her spleen by using the only resource available to her: making our lives miserable with noise, banging about her tiny kitchen, thumping around in her bedroom at odd hours of the day and night. Noisy housework at midnight was a perennial favourite.

'I'm gonna fucking go up there and sort 'er out,' Ginger

would threaten when Mary's banging and thumping reached crescendo levels. The poor construction and paper-thin walls of the flats made it very easy to create havoc this way – and Mary knew this, all too well. She'd managed to survive in her top-floor flat right through the Blitz – time enough to practise her banging and thumping act to perfection.

'Don't, Ging, she's a lonely old blind woman,' my mum would plead and, most of the time, my dad would relent and keep the peace. But there was the odd occasion when the noise from above would be too much, especially if it interrupted my dad's slumber. Then he'd stomp up the stairs in rage and hammer on her door.

'Whaddya bloody well think you're doin' you stupid cow! Stop that bloody bangin' or I'll 'ave the coppers on ya!'

This was, of course, an empty threat. Rousing the coppers of Dalston was not part of my dad's repertoire. And Mary didn't even come to the front door. Yet my dad's aggressive tactic was effective. The banging would stop, sometimes ceasing for weeks on end. Until the next time frustration at her existence would overwhelm her and the noise would start up again. Eventually, she moved out. Rumour had it she went into an old people's home, only to be replaced by an amorous young couple who spent most of their waking hours humping and grinding, puffing and panting, in their bedroom, creating an even more sensitive noise problem that was more or less impossible to resolve. (Even my dad would have baulked at climbing the stairs to yell, 'Stop bloody knockin' 'er off!')

The only neighbours we had anything to do with were the married age-gap couple in the flat next door. Harry, a skinny, moustachioed, somewhat seedy man in his fifties, a fancy-goods dealer, and his rather svelte blonde wife Sophie, whom he'd met at a West End dance hall just after the war.

Sophie was in her twenties, a half-Jewish refugee from Austria. And my mum became quite friendly with her over time; mainly, I suspect, because they had a common dislike of their environment – and couldn't quite understand how they'd wound up there.

Molly was convinced Sophie had married for reasons of security only.

'He did well during the war with the black market, so she must've thought he'd be a safe bet, what with having no family here and not wanting to go back to Austria.'

She was probably right. Yet the marriage, like other similar hasty liaisons of the time, was doomed to be quietly unhappy. Sophie was alone for much of the time – Harry frequently travelled around the country for work – and the pair had little in common. She fruitlessly craved the childhood joys of her cultural background, things like classical music and ballet; he preferred Vera Lynn and, later, Dickie Valentine records: you'd always know when Harry was back from a trip because you'd hear Vera belting out, 'There'll be Bluebirds Over The White Cliffs of Dover' from their front room. Harry had also made it plain he didn't want kids, so Sophie envied my mum, having a little girl to love and look after.

'I make a big mistake – and now I pay for it,' she'd tell Molly.

When Harry was away, Sophie initially babysat me for my parents a few times. But while my dad liked Harry, a fellow traveller in the East End world of ducking and diving, he had an uninhibited aversion to 'the German cow'. To my dad, there was no distinction between the Austrian and German population, even though Sophie said she'd come here to escape persecution. As far as he was concerned, they were all, men and women alike, tarred with the same brush. He even suspected Sophie's half-Jewish status was a ruse, to make her more acceptable as a refugee.

'Irma Grese was a woman,' he'd remind my mum if she tried to protest on behalf of her neighbour (Grese, executed for war crimes at the age of twenty two, had sadistically killed hundreds of inmates during her time as a warden at Belsen concentration camp), and in due course, Ginger stopped the babysitting.

'It's bad enough she's living next door,' was his rationale. 'I don't want her in my home looking after my kid.'

In fact, my dad didn't like anyone coming into our home. OK, it was small and damp and a tad depressing. But that wasn't the reason why I grew up in a place where we never entertained or rarely had visitors. The truth was, Ginger was somewhat possessive: he wanted his wife and kid right there, away from everything and everyone else.

No one, neighbour or relative, was actually invited into our home. Even when he wasn't there, my mum wasn't encouraged to invite people in for a cuppa or a chat. As I grew up, the only other person who'd come to our flat regularly would be Annie, our Irish cleaner.

Sarah, of course, had been around, visiting us occasionally after Ginger returned from India. But in 1947 she went off to live overseas permanently. And my mum's family had scattered, some abroad, the rest to other parts of the country. As for my dad's parents, we always went to them. They never ever came to us.

The one thing my dad couldn't control, however, was the unexpected occasional knock on the door out of the blue. Although we'd had a big black Bakelite phone in the living room from as far back as I could remember, many people then didn't have a home phone. So an unexpected knock on the door was a pretty normal occurrence for everyone else.

When we did get a rare, unheralded knock at the door from one of my mum's UK-based brothers, either bachelor Eddie (whom Ginger disliked because he was a habitual gambler and often on the scrounge) or Joe, my mum's favourite brother, who ran a gift shop in Brighton and had two daughters, my mum would be delighted. She'd rush into the kitchen, raid the larder and prepare all sorts of delicacies, egg or smoked-salmon sandwiches, teacakes, biscuits, drinks. Generous and open-hearted, she loved pulling out the stops to entertain for these unexpected rare visits; if my dad was there, he'd grit his teeth and keep up the façade of hospitality.

As for me, I was only used to being the sole focus of two people's lives and found such unexpected visits uncomfortable. I lived in the glow of my mum and dad's attention, taking it for granted that I was the centre of the entire universe. Adjusting to other people's company in the small confines of our flat, even briefly, seemed strange, an unhealthy beginning, which didn't do me any favours when it came to relating to others' needs later in life. So all I felt back then, once the visitors had departed and I'd been given the obligatory hug and kiss (which I hated: I was not a kissy-feely child) was an overwhelming sense of relief. 'I hope they don't come back,' the little voice inside me said. 'I don't like them coming round here.'

So while we rarely had visitors or neighbours over, in turn, my mum only ever ventured into Sophie's flat for tea and chats when my dad was at work. And in due course that stopped too – because of my dad's over-the-top feelings about the war. He wasn't alone in this, of course. If you've been bombed to smithereens, lost members of your family, spent years in army uniform or wound up a prisoner, you're bound to have strong opinions on what had happened. But holding a young, fairly innocent refugee woman responsible for the slaughter and destruction of millions of lives was a bit rich. Though I can see now, that it wasn't really just about the war.

As I said, my dad just didn't want anyone coming into our home.

CHAPTER 6
SUNDAYS

Sundays in post-war London were another planet away from the Sundays we now take for granted. Silent streets; virtually everything closed. Pubs open briefly at lunchtime and for a couple of hours at night. Everything else ground to a halt, apart from buses and trains. No supermarkets or round-the-clock shopping opportunities. People visited each other. Or they stayed indoors. And my early world was dominated by a late Sunday-afternoon routine that was unwavering in its rigidity: rain or shine, Molly and I would be required to pay homage to my father's parents, Miriam and Jack, a few miles away, just off Petticoat Lane in Stoney Lane. Ginger would eat his Sunday roast and then head for bed, sleeping off the week's rigours, preparing himself for the next. Sunday was the only night he was virtually sober.

Snug in my little beige wool coat with its velvet collar, a bow tied atop my frizzy curls, I'd clutch my mum's hand tightly as we headed down Shacklewell Lane, past the big synagogue and the hairdressers on the corner to wait for the 649 trolley bus ride that took us on the two-mile journey down Kingsland Road, past Shoreditch Church and Itchy Park (so named because of the tramps that used to doss there), down past Commercial Road and finally to Liverpool Street Station.

Increasingly nervous during the bus ride, my childish fear would start to become near panic, stomach churning, when we alighted outside Dirty Dick's pub. This was the truly horrible bit, the thing that gave me nightmares: the ten-minute walk through the near deserted Middlesex Street to Stoney Lane down the dark, narrow, dirty and eerie thoroughfares. At three years old, I'd absorbed much grown-up talk about the grisly, blood-splattered Victorian history of the area, mainly the Whitechapel Murders, when a series of young prostitutes were found murdered and horribly mutilated, many of these crimes reputed to have been committed by the knife of Jack The Ripper.

This gruesome gossip about the Ripper's ghastly slayings usually came from my grandmother, Miriam, probably because she and Jack lived just a few hundred yards away from The Bell, an ancient pub on Middlesex Street where, it was said, twenty-five-year-old prostitute Frances Coles, the last victim of the Whitechapel Murders, had drunk her final tipple with one of her clients in 1891. Hours later she'd been found, bleeding to death, her throat slashed, in a nearby street.

I only heard my grandmother tell this story to my mum once – but, unfortunately, I never ever forgot it.

'They say she was still alive when the copper found 'er. One of 'er eyes was still open,' Miriam told my mum with ghoulish relish.

Trotting along silently, still clutching my mum's hand tight, scary images like these would flash before me as we negotiated what had once been London's meanest streets of filth, poverty, prostitution and crime. Bomb damage and destruction all around the area made it even more sinister, if that were possible. So my imagination would be working overtime. What would happen to us if someone like The Ripper saw us as prey? Suppose they had a knife? We could try to run away. But would we be able to run fast enough?

Strangely, though, I kept these childish fears secret, unvoiced, on those scary Sunday trudges. The winters of those years were remarkable in their ferocity; there were killer smogs too: you'd open the front door and be confronted with a thick wall of yellow pollution. I learned to welcome such weather on a Sunday: my parents wouldn't consider taking me out anywhere if we hit one of those fogs or an exceptionally bad patch of wintry weather.

'Wanna go, wanna go,' I'd wail to my mum, stamping my tiny feet bad temperedly whenever we'd be obliged to go out on brief wintry sorties to shop for veggies at our nearby street market in Ridley Road. So she probably thought my silence on those Sunday walks down the Lane were due to my discomfort at the climate. Even if it wasn't raining, the late Sunday afternoon trudge always seemed to take place under grey, eerie, menacing skies.

Petticoat Lane Market itself, of course, had ceased the day's frenetic trading and was having its well-earned Sunday snooze: the streets and gutters littered with the detritus of market stalls, rotting fruit, near liquid vegetables, torn, muddy clothing, empty boxes and dirty newspaper wrappings.

Legend had it you could buy anything you wanted in the Lane and years later, a friend told me that once, she'd seen two lion cubs for sale there – but I remained permanently disinterested in what the Lane had to offer. To an over-imaginative toddler, this was a murky, fear-filled, dark Dickensian world of grotesque horror. Only infrequent childhood trips to underground stations could match this place as a source of fear in my troubled imagination. Over time, this fear developed into a lifelong abhorrence of dark, enclosed, claustrophobic places. Just one childhood visit to the Angel underground station, where we stood on a platform that was, effectively, a terrifyingly narrow concrete strip with tube trains rattling past us on either side of the strip, was enough to give me endless nightmares as a kid.

Jack and Miriam lived in what they liked to call 'the buildings' in Stoney Lane, ancient apartment dwellings with stone stairs and a strange, unidentifiable smell. This sour aroma of a poorly ventilated, tightly inhabited building remained so vivid, so powerful in my memory that decades later, in Sydney, visiting a friend who had just moved into an inner-city apartment in an old building, I smelt that same strange stale stench as I climbed the stairs. 'Yeah, it's the smell of the buildings,' said my friend, a cockney artist from south London. 'I remember it too from when I was a kid.'

For my grandparents, life in 'the buildings' was everything

they wanted: they loved being part of the neighbourhood, surrounded by people they'd known for years, a community that remained tight and close, heedless of its dismal, squalid backdrop; here every stallholder, every shopkeeper knew each other, could recite everyone's history, family, working lives, troubles. It was a lawless place too, of course. My father's family weren't crims but came from a long line of duckers and divers. In the Lane, the law was something you could often sidestep, usually with a bung (bribe) in the right place.

Years later, when a well-meaning attempt was made by the Corporation of London authority to rehouse my grandparents, to what is now the Barbican, in the post-war building boom, they refused. Incredible. Perhaps it was an age thing: they were well into their sixties by the time the war ended. Change, comfort and an improved vista held no interest for them. They loved what they knew.

Slowly, resentfully, we'd climb the stairs to their home. They rented what were actually two separate flats on one floor; one flat, kept for family members on overnight stays, had an infrequently used dining room plus a spare bedroom with a scullery on the landing outside. The landing also boasted a toilet cubicle, complete with wooden seat. Newspaper was deployed to wipe yourself: the scratchy Izal paper in its square pack that we used at home was too posh for my grandparents, even though they weren't short of cash. On the other side of the landing were Miriam and Jack's main living quarters, a smallish living room-cum-kitchen with a bedroom behind.

Miriam, stern and white-haired with a pink, unblemished skin, wearing shapeless floral garments, usually covered by some sort of apron, and with a razor sharp tongue, would always have a cake ready for our teatime visit: usually a round plain cake with white icing on the top from Kossoff's bakery nearby.

Miriam was a toughie, she'd raised five kids in the area while working full time alongside Jack in their Middlesex Street coal shop – my dad, the eldest, was virtually raised by Miriam's sisters. Her language was colourful, peppered with four-letter words and the odd bit of Jewish slang.

'Your Jackie's a little rech (pronounced rosh),' she'd frequently tell my mum. 'But I like a kid with a bit of spirit.'

In its Yiddish translation, the word means a devil, hardly a polite observation but she had a point: my temper tantrums if things weren't going my way could be quite spectacular, though I reserved my best ones for home. For me, the only joy of those visits was the cake, the highlight of the whole exercise. Even if it did sit on a rather odd tablecloth, made up from last week's newspapers.

Somewhat incongruously, a copy of *The Tatler*, the glossy magazine for toffs, would often be lying on the newspaper tablecloth. Miriam's tastes were eclectic: she was immersed in the ghoulishness and gore of the Lane's history, yet she also devoured *The Tatler* each month, the *Hello!* magazine of its day, vicariously relishing the somewhat extreme contrast between her world and that of the country's privileged classes. (The newspaper tablecloth is an unsolved mystery; they could certainly afford to buy a decent tablecloth. Probably it was sheer perversity on my grandmother's part, along with the rejection of paid-for toilet paper.)

The visits mostly involved my mum chatting to Miriam

across the teacups, while I usually wriggled impatiently in the chair, licking the last crumbs of cake from my fingers and waiting longingly for a second or third slice to be dished onto my plate. Like my dad, my grandfather would lie sleeping for most of Sunday afternoon, so conversation was usually limited to my grandmother moaning, mostly about Jack, to whom she was fervently attached, Superglue like, often following him down to the nearby pub, The Bell, to try to drag him away from the bar if she suspected other women were eyeing him up. Miriam was five years older than Jack. Perhaps it was the Toyboy Syndrome that made her so possessive, so fearful of losing him to another woman's embrace.

Whatever lay behind her passion for Jack, this fierce, overwhelming obsession with her hubby's doings had actually brought them to this flat, right at the beginning of the war, just before the Blitz.

In the thirties, Miriam and Jack continued to run their shop on Middlesex Street but, like many other Jewish people who ran businesses there, opted to move away from the market to a house, complete with garden and dog, in Clapton, a few miles away and much more pleasant. But her increasing jealousy of her husband led Miriam to insist that the couple move back to the area to live in 'the buildings' once their sons were in the army and their daughters evacuated, so that she could keep a close eye on Jack in the shop, which was now turned into a commission agent's office.

Thousands of people were fleeing London, heading to safer parts of the country. But Miriam chose the reverse, moving even closer to the heart of the city – and the impossible-to-ignore danger from the Luftwaffe's bombs – such was her need to watch over her beloved. And there they stayed.

If Miriam wasn't moaning or complaining about Jack, she'd usually start dissing my father's nightly drinking habits to my mum.

'Go through 'is pockets, Molly, when he passes out, and take what money you want,' was Miriam's tip, culled from a lifetime's experience of pickpocketing her spouse.

''E'll be so drunk he'll never remember what he 'ad – and at least it won't be goin' down the drain in the pub.'

I don't believe my mother ever took her advice. My dad was generous, she had whatever she wanted – and she hadn't grown up in a world where it was acceptable to surreptitiously take money out of a loved-one's wallet, though clearly in Petticoat Lane the rules of domestic life had to be adapted to the circumstances: Jack was far from the only boozer or gambler in town.

Sometimes there'd be other visitors joining us at the newspaper-covered table: my father's lively dark-haired sister Deirdre, and her son, Anthony, two years older than me and a pale, shy kid. We did not click, Anthony and I. He too was an only child, pampered by his mum and beautifully turned out, a right little Lord Fauntleroy in tiny tailored suits and cute little bow ties. Deirdre made all his clothes.

But he had made something of an enemy of me right from the start: at one of our early encounters in the Stoney Lane flat, he'd unexpectedly thrown up at the table – and managed to be sick all over my little buckskin shoes. Molly was horrified. I started wailing. Deirdre dragged him, his trousers covered in sick, outside to the loo. My grandmother seemed to enjoy the unexpected diversion as she helped Molly mop up my shoes and socks: a never-to-be-forgotten, oft recounted family moment.

Anthony also seemed to have a morbid fascination with the adult conversation. Mutely, he'd sit there, ears flapping, taking in every word. I wasn't especially interested in what the adults said or did; I was far too focused on my own preoccupations, which were usually along the lines of 'When can we go home?' once the cake had been demolished.

Occasionally, Jack, or The Old Man, as my parents called him, would emerge from the bedroom and join us. Round faced with big black-framed glasses, he was an amiable if gruff sort of man. I wasn't a spontaneously affectionate kid and never attempted to openly woo or charm either of my grandparents: they weren't exactly the cuddly sort and to me, at that stage, they were kindly but nonetheless unappealing figures, mainly because I sensed, even then, that they were East End toughies of the old school and I recoiled, through over-sensitivity, from the harshness of this dark world they were so attached to.

So it tended to be cousin Anthony who would play up to his granddad and ask to play with his fob watch, schooled by his mum to 'be nice to gramps' in order to be rewarded with a parting gift of a pound note or two. Back home later, after another scary walk through the Lane's dark, deserted streets to the bus home, my fears somewhat tempered by relief that it was nearly over, my mum would comment on this to my dad.

'You should have seen the way Anthony was schmoozing The Old Man today,' she'd tell my dad, who was as equally immersed in family politics as he was in the rigours of betting six days a week. 'It made me sick the way he was playing up to him. Jac would never crawl round anyone like that.'

She was dead right there. Crawling round anyone for a quick quid was definitely not an option. And by now, little Jac was mighty relieved to be back in the damp, pokey, familiar space of our flat. For now, all thoughts of The Ripper, the Lane and the strange newspaper tablecloth could be banished from my mind. Until Sunday afternoon came around again…

CHAPTER 7

A LIBERTY
BODICE

Wherever you were living in the freezing snowbound British winter of '47, you were probably cold.

To add insult to injury, there was a fuel crisis. Coal – the source of heat for many – was in short supply because the roads and railways were blocked by heavy snow. Stockpiles at depots or pits froze and could not be moved for weeks. (Central heating was pretty much unheard of.) The roads got so bad, transport sometimes stopped completely. Power cuts were frequent, even radio broadcasts were kept brief. Without candles in the house, you were stuffed.

People were frequently heard to mutter, 'this is worse than the bleedin' war' as they huddled at home or in the streets, wearing as many warm clothes as they could lay their hands on. In some cases, people worked in their offices by candlelight and high-street shops were lit by candles and gas lamps. And if you think that sounds romantic, forget it. Going outside could be treacherous. Even when the snow melted, the icy slush meant it could be perilous just venturing across a main road.

With my dad's cash and contacts we'd managed to stockpile extra bags of coal in the bathroom cupboard for such emergencies. The little fireplaces in the flat had fires going constantly, which kept us warm but didn't do much for our health, given the amount of coal dust generated.

People wore quite heavy outer clothes, woollen coats, suits, to protect themselves – men and women alike frequently wore hats or scarves as streetwear – but for children, serious protection from the cold meant piling on as many warm clothes as possible plus paying close attention to underwear. Especially the liberty bodice.

We are in my parents' bedroom. A coal fire smoulders in the tiny grate and Molly is unsuccessfully trying to dress me.

'Don' wanna!' I scream at her, flinging the hated object across the room.

'Don' wanna wear it!'

'It'll keep you warm, Jac,' my mum pleads, managing to pull a cream-coloured, scratchy woollen vest down over my head to tuck into my knickers.

I wriggle away. Now I'm doing my perennial devil's dance, running round the bedroom, screaming myself silly. To say I was a tantrum-prone kid is putting it mildly. I was a screamer. And a persistent one at that.

'Not gonna wear it! Naaaah!'

The object in question, the liberty bodice, is a sleeveless garment made from a warm fleecy material with rubber buttons all the way down, a Victorian creation that has survived the first half of the twentieth century. The general idea was to wear it over a woolly vest for extra protection from colds and coughs. Some believed it was a kind of insurance against nastier, more life-threatening illnesses, like pneumonia. So, not surprisingly, Molly is desperate for me to wear it. But I nearly always reject it, mainly because I hate the rubber buttons, which go squidgy in the wash. And it takes ages to do up. (Patience is a virtue I can only admire in others.)

'OK,' she sighs, picking it up and putting it into a drawer, letting me win for the sake of peace and quiet. 'Let's get the rest of your things on.'

During those winters, as I went from toddler to school child, getting me to wear a liberty bodice was just one of the many everyday hassles my mum coped with. Because, like many kids, I was constantly poorly.

Bronchitis was an annual event, backed up intermittently by the usual childhood ailments like measles, mumps and whooping cough. Fortunately, the arrival of the new National Health Service in the summer of 1948 meant that we had our 'panel' doctor, Dr Kinglin, just a short walk away in Sandringham Road. (GPs then were known as 'panel' doctors because they were entitled to be on the panel or committee of those providing care under the new National Insurance Act of Parliament.) And all kids eventually got vaccinated for real nasties like TB and polio, which was a really big worry in the 50s. But despite the authorities' attempts to boost children's welfare, while ours was a home of plenty nutritionally, the combination of damp walls and coal fires meant it wasn't exactly healthy.

My dad's health too had been damaged from his time in the

hot, humid climate of India, where he'd contracted malaria. In the early years after he'd returned, recurring bouts of the illness came on suddenly, without warning. He'd start shivering, throwing up and get bad headaches. The attacks would leave him exhausted, bed-bound and sweating profusely. My mum would have to change the sheets and put them through the kitchen mangle because they were literally drenched in his sweat. Over time, the malaria attacks lessened. The bottles of quinine tablets in the bathroom cabinet had not been very effective in preventing these incidents. But he kept them, just in case. Alongside the bottles of Eno Salts and Andrews Liver Salts, which he regularly used to help cure his morning-after hangovers.

Those coal fires inside, of course, didn't help when you considered the terrible fogs and smogs outside, essentially really bad pollution which plagued London's streets for many years after the war until The Clean Air Act 1956 restricted the pollution with the introduction of smoke-free zones where only smokeless fuels like coke could be burned. At one point before the cleanup, the pea-soupers were so bad and visibility so poor in London's streets that bus conductors were reduced to walking in front of the bus with a flashlight; an estimated 12,000 people died in London as a consequence of the Great Smog of 1952.

The coal fires, of course, had a dual purpose for families: you huddled round them for warmth, but you also habitually dried your clothes in front of them, thereby absorbing more smoke into your body. And, though we didn't think or know about it at the time, my dad's smoking habit, twenty Players a day, plus the odd cigar, all contributed to the general unhealthy fug all around us: my mum too became prone to bouts of bronchitis.

And so it was regular Vicks VapoRub, Friar's Balsam (an inhalant), and Eno cough syrup, the main products widely available to ease congestion. And if things got bad, the new 'wonder drugs' like penicillin had emerged via the NHS to combat chest or lung infection, which actually saved my life – and probably many others – during the foggy early winter months of 1948.

I'm in my parents' bed, semiconscious but vaguely aware of the strangeness of the situation: by now, at age three, my permanent sleeping place is the little front bedroom. But they've moved me. It's serious.

Anxiously, Molly and Ginger creep in and out to watch over me, voices hushed, their faces grave. A nasty cough has suddenly turned into a fever. I toss and turn, burning hot one minute, teeth chattering the next. So they nervously call Dr Kinglin.

'It's pneumonia,' he says gravely, after examining me, his stethoscope cold and probing against my clammy skin. 'To be honest, Mrs Hyams, it's touch and go,' he adds, handing my mum a prescription for the penicillin.

'Get her to take this and if she makes it through the next twenty-four hours, she'll be OK.'

And so, for those perilous twenty-four hours, they take it in turns to catch some sleep in the small bedroom while the other holds vigil over my bedside, somehow coaxing me to swallow the precious drugs – luckily, the chemist in the High Street was open – sip water or a few precious spoonfuls of soup before I drift off again.

'Thank you for the hankies, Daddy,' I tell Ginger at one point.

I am delirious, raving, my dreams have somehow morphed into a surreal reality. How scared they must be, how powerless they must feel in the face of this unexpected calamity. Oblivious to all fear, I sleep through most of the night. And, the following morning, just as the doctor has predicted, my temperature has dropped, the fever has gone and the delirium has vanished. I'm out of the woods.

But it's several weeks before I am fully recovered and they dare to take me out again. 'Those drugs,' they tell anyone who will listen, 'they really are wonder drugs, you know.' And their trust, in the doctors, the NHS, this amazing new system of free healthcare for everyone, is formed for the rest of their lives.

If I was cherished and mollycoddled by my parents before this frightening event, it reached epic proportions afterwards, understandable perhaps for an only child, but it eventually left me feeling uncomfortable and, later on, somewhat frustrated.

Sadly, you sometimes hear people say that they never felt really loved by one or both parents. My problem was the reverse: I always knew I was loved and was the centre of two people's entire universe, yet the older I got, the more I felt stifled by this overprotectiveness, this fear that harm might come to me, especially via the harsh elements outside the 'safety' of our flat.

Yet the bout of pneumonia had another, more positive outcome. Fully aware that I'd diced with death, overhearing my mum's phone conversations about it, I became more compliant when my mum suggested I don the dreaded liberty bodice in the winter months. Soon, I was insisting on buttoning it up myself. I continued to wear it throughout my childhood. Though to this day, the very thought of those rubber buttons still has the power to make me shudder.

CHAPTER 8
THE ASCOT'S REVENGE

There was a Monster living in our little flat. It had quite a bit of competition, mind you, from the other less-than-appealing aspects of our home. It competed with the damp paper-thin walls – giving me ample opportunity, in my cramped bedroom, to hear my parents performing their daily rituals – the slash-your-wrists-now view from the pocket-sized kitchen (a bombsite that eventually became a very noisy timberyard), and the equally grim vista from my parents' bedroom and living room – a somewhat sinister sloping tiled roof of what had once been a dairy in Shacklewell Lane.

The Monster resided in the bathroom, attached to the wall, a smart, shiny white enamel contraption with a blue triangle triumphantly proclaiming its heritage: the Ascot, the 'water heater' that didn't, couldn't, wouldn't deliver the one thing you desperately wanted – constant running hot water for a bath.

Living with the Monster was an unending battle that went on for years: the on-off pilot light versus my mum. My parents were very proud of it the day the man from the Gas Board came round and installed it over the bath. Essentially, the Monster was a small gas water heater with a spout emerging directly from it. The heater was ignited from a pilot light inside when you wanted to run the tap for hot water. Those modern-day miracles cost about £10 each at the time – a few hundred pounds in today's terms – so Molly considered herself lucky to have one in the bathroom. Kitchen hot water still came from saucepans heated on the gas cooker.

Ascots were relatively new then. Introduced into Britain in the late thirties by a German company, for many people they were the first ever source of hot water 'on tap', so it's nice to know that our country's triumph over Hitler came with a nasty domestic sting in its tail: all over the land, families like ours in the post-war years regularly did battle with the temperamental device and its unpredictable on-off pilot light.

The general idea was that you'd light the pilot light inside the Ascot with the manual push switch underneath. Then, in theory, the light would go on, ready to heat up the water. Alas, when you let go of the manual switch, the light would all too frequently flicker, weaken – and go off. So no hot water.

'The pipe's blocked up,' said the man from the North Thames Gas Board when my mum managed to get him round after we'd valiantly endured our first lengthy running battle with the Ascot, hours of torture which resulted in nothing more than a cold bath.

After what seemed like ages tinkering in the bathroom, he announced that he'd 'done his best'.

'If it keeps going out again, you could try lighting it yourself with a match,' was his passing shot, a pretty useless piece of advice because it still didn't work. Time and again, he'd come round, tinker and leave, whistling his way down the dirty stone stairs, his pockets bulging with my dad's cash, our yearning for hot water on tap still largely unfulfilled. Since neither of my parents had a clue about anything remotely practical around the home we were, of course, sitting ducks for this 'oooh, gonna cost ya' type of situation.

And so the nightly bathtime ritual when I was aged five or thereabouts went something like this. I'd stand there in the little bathroom in my pyjamas, watching and waiting, heart in mouth, as Molly, ever the optimist, would gingerly turn the manual push switch on. Ginger never got involved. He'd still be out 'at work' (a euphemism for the George and Dragon pub) most nights.

Whooosh! The blue light had come on! Carefully, not daring to believe her luck, my mum would then turn the tap on. First a trickle, then a gush, yes! It was hot water! The prospect of a lovely hot bath, with me splashing around in delight, had me hopping up and down in anticipation.

'Mum, Mum, it's working, it's working,' I'd chirp.

But my innocent joy was frequently short-lived. For, as we eventually learned, life with the Monster was never going to be as simple as that. Gradually, it dawned on us that once we'd watched the trickle turn to a flood, we could never risk leaving the bathroom to happily assume the flow of hot water from the Monster would result in a steaming hot bath. The Monster was far too cunning for that. If we stepped out to just leave it to its job, the Monster took umbrage. And it promptly stopped heating the water. All too often we'd nip back to the bathroom to find the light out, the water now tepid. Over and over again, our dreams of a hot bath were a fiasco, a disaster. The Monster was spiteful. It toyed with our hopes, our dreams, in a sadistic way. For while there were times when it let us have what we wanted, all too often the Monster won the war of nerves and didn't perform. Welcome to the Ascot's Revenge.

And so I grew up understanding that to be really sure of a decent hot bath there was only one true way: you deployed endless saucepans of heated water, dashing back and forth between the kitchen and the bathroom (one advantage of having such a pokey flat meant there was virtually no distance between the two), tipping the hot water into the bath, then running back again to collect another saucepan from the kitchen to fill with more cold water to be heated. This, of course, took some time because the gas cooker took ages to warm the pans.

In my early years, Mum would give up trying to get the Ascot to work and with a sigh, she would get the matches, light the gas on the kitchen cooker, and wait for the saucepan to boil to make me a bath. (Like many of their generation, my parents grew up with the 'strip wash' over a basin full of warmed-up water, so my little baths, somehow, tended to take precedence over their own requirements.)

Then, as I grew bigger, I was allowed to 'make' the nightly bath myself, carefully taking each heated saucepan into the bathroom to slosh it into the bath, nervously testing the hot water to see how much cold I could add to move things along and allow me get into the bath to finally splash around.

Only when I'd reached my early teens did things improve, and better, more efficient water heaters were installed in the kitchen and bathroom, as well as new gas fires that replaced the coal fires in the other rooms. But for me, bathtime as a kid will always be associated with trying to wash myself in a less-than-satisfactory amount of tepid water, always watched by the white Monster over the bath and the flickering pilot light, taunting me endlessly with their power.

CHAPTER 9
A DIAMOND RING

Not everyone in our street was as involved as we were in acquiring goods via the thriving black market through the early post-war years. The family who inhabited the condemned house on the corner, the Coopers, and their boy Bobby, or our downstairs' neighbour Maisie in the ground-floor flat, weren't likely to splurge on any of the black-market luxuries found in our home: you needed hard cash to continuously take advantage of it.

While the post-war black market still prevailed across the country, in London's Petticoat Lane, the city's oldest, established, unruly trading post, it boomed. All sorts of things found their way to the Lane, virtually everything you couldn't officially buy in those times of lean living, to be sold with a nudge and a wink: ciggies, nylons, off-ration expensive clothing, small items of furniture, booze and all kinds of tinned foods were frequently available – right up until the time rationing officially ended in 1954.

In my dad's bookie world of punters, spivs and runners,

ignoring the regulations and using black-market goods to trade for favours was as normal as going to the pub, picking up bets and boozing.

Big bottles of whisky, expensive French perfume, packs of shiny seamed stockings, tins of red salmon or canned sliced peaches, different kinds of cosmetics, soaps and toiletries frequently found their way into our little flat, luxuries my mother soon took for granted, along with the large wooden boxes of the finest Havana cigars that took pride of place on our mantelpiece, or the curved white containers with brightly coloured plastic labels containing exotica like sticky dates, that sometimes piled up in our pantry.

Even with coupons, you couldn't buy these things freely in the shops. But Ginger frequently reached for his wad of cash to peel off a few notes for such items when they were offered to him by stallholders or drinking pals, even if we didn't really need them. Sometimes, of course, we wouldn't see the things he had purchased in our home: they'd form part of a trade-off for a favour my dad had done or owed someone.

But while passing over black-market goods as tips was one thing, my dad had a consistent habit of getting whatever he wanted: the 'bung', cockney slang for a bribe, cash slipped into the right hand to open a hitherto closed door or facilitate a favour. Bungs were a way of life on his territory.

My dad used the bung in various ways. He was a generous tipper too, beloved by the cabbies who brought him home nightly, but primarily, his philosophy was using the bung to cut all corners, get you whatever you wanted or needed fast. And because you'd paid for a favour in cash, you could always come back for another – with yet another bung, of course.

As a child, of course, I had no real idea what this really meant; I just heard about it, absorbed it in passing chat between my parents. The legendary world of the poverty stricken East End – where everyone had very little, but helped each other out just the same – didn't seem to operate that way in our case. Virtually everything my dad did was a trade-off; favours were always paid for in hard cash.

So while much of the country scrimped, saved, queued and generally endured a bleak, miserable post-war landscape, people like my dad were living it large after the war, simply because they always had the 'readies'. And, of course, this time was very much a cash culture, though my dad was a big fan of the relationship forged with the bank manager – and postdated cheques. The bank manager too was a frequent recipient of my dad's largesse. Frequent double scotches in the pub and the well-placed supply of boxes of Havanas were another way of cementing the 'nudge, nudge, wink, wink' relationship.

Officially, my dad and The Old Man ran the formal side of their business from their tiny office, taking telephone bets from customers who ran an account with them. But the lucrative side, of course, was taking cash bets on the street or in the pub, helped by their small team of trusted 'runners'. A lot of this illicit exchange of cash and betting slips actually went on in the men's toilet in the pub.

This way of life, while not actually observed by myself or my mum, still got absorbed into our home life. Knowing and hearing about it as I grew up made me streetwise, to an extent, because all around me the official rules were being broken – with no obvious consequences. But there was one consequence – I grew up with the somewhat warped idea that if anyone did you a favour, big or small, somehow you 'owed' that individual, even if the favour was given carelessly or meant little to the other person at the time. You never forgot that personal debt. One good turn deserves another, certainly. But not for ever.

This distorted belief dominated my life far into adulthood. I firmly believed that if someone did you a personal favour, you were indebted to them. This meant that I was unable to clearly discriminate between a genuine gesture of helpfulness or friendship and one which was primarily made out of self interest, unhelpful, to say the least, in the cut and thrust world of journalism where 'scratch my back and I'll scratch yours' behaviour is all pervasive. Time and again I'd be shocked to realise how misplaced I'd been in my belief that certain individuals were 'friends' because of one helpful, spontaneous gesture which, while I'd clung to it as proof of friendship or loyalty, merely turned out to be directly related to my place in the editorial pecking order. Yet only quite recently did I fully realise where this misplaced view came from. Maybe there were a few genuine cash-free favours around us when I was a child. But I never saw evidence of this.

Yet there was one memorable occasion when what fell off the back of a lorry, or came into our home from heaven knows where, really did make a big impact on my child's view of my dad's wheeling and dealing. It was the night he came home from the George & Dragon with a big diamond ring in his pocket.

'Len-from-the-caff said it was about time I got you one of

these,' said Ginger, producing a small black velvet box from his jacket pocket and plonking it down, without ceremony, on the living room table.

Len, one of my dad's older cronies who liked a bet or two, had known my father's family for years because he ran a busy little café near their shop. He also knew that my parents had had a rushed register office wedding the year after the war started – and that as a consequence, my mum had never had a proper engagement ring.

'So this is it, Mol, your engagement ring,' said my dad with some pride.

The words were hardly out of his mouth when my mum reached out to prise open the little black box and remove the sparkling object.

'Oh it's GORGEOUS,' she cooed, setting the ring on her finger and holding it out with considerable delight.

'And it's so BIG'. I daren't go out with it around here, Ging. The neighbours would have a fit if they saw it. Still… I can wear it for that big wedding next month, can't I?'

'Course you can, Mol,' shrugged my dad, heading for the bedroom to change out of his suit into his pyjamas, his nightly after-work ritual.

Typically, nothing was said about what he'd paid for the ring or where it came from. In all likelihood, the ring had been passed to him as collateral by a hard-up punter who'd had some serious losses; probably, the punter, desperate for something to trade, had nicked it from his own wife or girlfriend's jewellery stash without her knowledge. (The world of the heavy gambler is defined by such acts of spontaneity, as anyone who has lived with a compulsive gambler will confirm.) Len was probably just the saloon bar 'middleman', encouraging my dad to take the ring, rather than wait for the cash he was owed, which after all, might never materialise.

But my mother was not troubled by the ring's provenance. She was far too delighted to concern herself with the details. The next morning, she was on the phone to her best friend from schooldays, Evelyn, regaling her with the news.

'Wait till you see it, Eve, it's the real McCoy,' she trilled. 'I'm sure it's worth hundreds.'

Evelyn was not impressed. She didn't like Ginger one bit. A single mum with a small son, born after a brief wartime fling with a pilot, she had to live with the somewhat difficult status of unmarried mum which, in those days, carried a heavy penalty of social condemnation, even though illegitimacy rates had soared during the war years. So the official cover-up story was that Evelyn's 'husband' had 'gone to live in Canada'.

Evelyn accepted her lot. But she still resented the fact that while she had to slog away, six days a week, in her brother's West End shop, my mum didn't need to work. Ginger, according to Evelyn, was a n'er-do-well with a shady livelihood. In reality, of course, the two women were in a similar boat, coping as best they could with what life had dished out to them in the aftermath of war. In fact, Evelyn's wealthy brother had helped her with the down payment on a small house in the suburbs. So to some degree she could look down on Molly, stuck in a pokey Dalston slum with a boozy street bookie, while she struggled to bring up her illegitimate son respectably in a Neasden semi.

'Did you ask him where he got it from?' enquired Evelyn,

who was always ultra bitchy when the conversation turned to my dad.

'Why should I?' said Molly, undaunted. 'It's a diamond ring and I know he paid for it.'

'How can you be sure?' snapped Evelyn. 'I'd watch it if I were you, wearing something like that without knowing where he got it from.'

'Ginger's not a thief, Evelyn,' was Molly's parting shot. 'Anyway, I'm going now, just wanted to tell you my news. Bye!'

Conversations with Evelyn frequently ended this way. Her bitterness at her tough situation soured their exchanges. And my mum, kind and easy-going, was a moving target for her friend's sharp tongue. Yet Evelyn was cannier than my mother, who blithely took each day as it came. And she was right – you could never be too sure what kind of shenanigan was going on with my dad. And, true to form, my mum's new-found delight in actually owning a big diamond sparkler wasn't destined to last very long.

Two days later, my dad came home from work and said he had to take the ring back. He gave no reason.

'I'm sorry, Mol,' he consoled my crestfallen mother. 'I'll get you another one, promise. But you can't have this one.'

Who knows what the dodgy deal had involved? Maybe my dad needed to quickly trade the ring for cash himself. There were occasionally times when he placed his own bets and lost heavily, so then he needed to replenish his wad of cash quickly to keep working, though he could always rely on The Old Man for cash if his own stash ran down. Maybe, this time, he just didn't want to ask for a helpful handout. There were often fallings-out and rows in The George and Dragon with The Old Man that we heard about in snatches.

My own theory is that my dad had consumed several large Scotches when he did the deal via Len-from-the-caff and took possession of the ring – and in the cold light of dawn, had mulled it over and decided to turn it back into cash as quickly as he could. Knowing my dad, he may even have lost on the deal.

All I knew then was that he reneged on his big promise: my mum never got a diamond ring from my dad again. But typically, she didn't complain or start bawling him out, not when he took the little black box from her or even afterwards. She said nothing, just took it all in her stride and got on with the routine of her life, fussing around me, dressing me beautifully, cooking our meals, making sure she looked svelte and immaculate before taking me out and about on Kingsland Road.

Those grey years with their power cuts, food shortages, fogs and freezing winters seem overwhelmingly drab and wretched nowadays. But my mum's bright, positive, uncomplaining nature ignored the backdrop – and the worst of my dad's rackety behaviour. And, of course, she never had to worry about bills or money: my father's cash stash continued to see to all that.

Throughout my childhood, Ginger walked about every day with considerable sums of money in his pocket as he went about his bookie business. On some occasions it would run into the hundreds. Had he seriously considered it, he could easily have afforded to buy my mother a piece of good jewellery after a good week's takings or a big win. Over time, my mum did acquire a few nice things in her jewellery box – a pearl necklace and a couple of decent watches. But no gold or diamond rings. For while he was generous and incredibly free and easy with the cash in his hand, it never occurred to him to put any of his money into something that might endure – or, indeed, be of value if times got tough.

When you consider that in 1955, an eight-room house in Victoria Park, Hackney could be purchased for £2,000, with a deposit of £175 – a sum my dad would probably blow in the pub during a few weeks' heavy drinking with punters – it's clear that the opportunities were always there for him to improve our lives and give us a more spacious, pleasant environment. A thirties suburban house outside London with a garden cost more, say £3,500 back then. But even this he could have easily afforded, both deposit and repayments.

Certainly, the street bookie of that era always needed cash for punters, bungs and, in my dad's case, big rounds in the pub. Yet that, for him, was enough. It all stopped there. Things like mortgages, insurance policies, even savings accounts didn't exist for my dad, probably because his father didn't 'believe' in such things. Even with his clerical worker's background, working with figures, adding up day in, day out (personal calculators were unknown then) he just didn't see any merit in looking ahead financially. And Molly never ever nagged him to make any changes; they both lived for the here and now. Perhaps this was a consequence of coming through the uncertainty and fears of war. But I suspect it was also to do with their personalities; in that way they were well matched.

So that's the story of how my mum nearly got to own a diamond ring.

She did get a mink coat, mind you. But that was decades later, after my dad had died. And yes, you guessed it – she paid for it herself. With a credit card.

CHAPTER 10
A RAT'S TALE

My dad's betting business thrived in the post-war betting frenzy: fivers and tenners aplenty for all. We acquired a retinue of 'servants' on my dad's payroll: Annie, our Irish cleaner, The Old Man's chauffeur, Dave, to drive us around in a big posh Daimler on family outings or holidays at the seaside, Renee, our regular babysitter, plus the ongoing services of a couple of my dad's runners who doubled up as delivery men to bring us anything we needed, mostly in the food department, direct from the Lane to our front door.

The oldest and most trusted of these, Wag, was somewhat odd. My mum said he looked like a tramp and, indeed, he was pretty unappealing: a fag end permanently clamped to his lips, his long, thin face grey and pockmarked, his attire shabby – usually a long, grey, belted and very tatty overcoat and a flat cap that always covered his head, rain or shine.

I'd sometimes hide behind my mum, peering at Wag in fascination, when she opened the door to take bag after bag of the provisions he had lugged on the bus from the Lane for us.

There was little dialogue. My mum would say thanks and Wag would grunt an indecipherable response. He never came in, of course, whatever the weather.

My mum, always fanatical about appearances, would complain about him to Ginger.

'Does he ever wash, Ging? He looks a bit...pongy.'

'Dunno,' my dad would shrug.

''E's worked for The Old Man for years. Never bin known to nick anything.'

These deliveries were usually on a Friday, so my mum could be ready to embark on a big weekend cooking spree, frying all different kinds of fish – halibut, salmon, plaice – preparing big roasting chickens, or unwrapping big joints of beef, peeling potatoes to roast, shelling peas, slicing up cabbages and carrots. They were meals we didn't always manage to finish because there was always far too much for two adults and a child; cold cooked food is one of my strongest memories of childhood.

My parents were also stepping out regularly by now, enjoying themselves in those years around 1947-1949 when London started to emerge from its blackout curtain, This meant Big Nights Out with my dad's cronies, going to shows, boxing matches, often getting the best seats for the latest West-End musical. Sometimes my dad would be given free tickets to shows by generous punters so off they'd go in a taxi, all dressed up, my dad in his latest sharp double-breasted suit, my mum in one of her slinky wrapover beaded crepe numbers, worn with platform shoes, hair piled high.

One day Molly told me they'd gone to see *Oklahoma*, the first of the big post-war Broadway musicals to open in the

West End and, amazingly, they'd wound up sitting yards away from the Queen and Prince Philip. Only she was Princess Elizabeth back then, a few years before her coronation in 1953.

'Oh she's so beautiful, the Princess,' my mum purred. 'You should see her skin, perfect, like porcelain. They just came in and sat down two rows in front of us. We couldn't believe it.'

I was young, but this royal glamour, tiaras and ermine, left an impression on me. The austerity years were somewhat glitter deficient. Real glamour, for the masses, was at a premium. Footballers then weren't a part of the celebrity circus; even big players earned very little, a maximum of £20 a week, until things started to change in the early sixties. There were movie stars, of course – in the early fifties, the UK version of the American *Photoplay* magazine gave glamour-hungry movie fans a chance to pore over sepia-tinted photos and stories of the big stars of the day like Tony Curtis, Grace Kelly, Lana Turner, Burt Lancaster and many others. Yet the British Royal Family, buoyed by the huge wave of support they'd garnered from the public during the war, continued to be objects of near worship then, especially with images of a young, beautiful princess inheriting the throne with a tall, blonde and handsome young naval lieutenant by her side.

TV images, of course, weren't around yet; like everyone else, we didn't actually acquire a television until the Coronation. So my pre-pubescent obsessions with imagery focused strongly on the two-and-sixpenny best-selling hardback picture books of these glittering, distant creatures at their wedding, with their children and at the big Coronation.

Those photographic images in the pre-Diana/celeb years were equally as powerful, in their way, as the tidal wave of celebrity images we now receive. People needed something glittery and highly costumed to admire then, to look up to, to gaze at in awe and wonder, in total contrast to the grey world of queues and shortages. It was a perfect antidote to the miserable times, helping people forget all about the bleakness of the grey skies, the sheer slog of living. Even if it was a bit ridiculous, worshipping a privileged group of unknown people in ermine who remained firmly on a distant pedestal. But of course, the very mystique of that far-off royal world was what hooked you in the first place…

Money was also thrown at my early 'education'. Because I was chattering away as a tiny tot, developing an aptitude for words and picking up the alphabet, clearly hungry to learn, my mum enrolled me at an expensive kindergarten for pre-school kids on Stamford Hill, a couple of miles away.

Twice a week she would take me there on the bus and I began to read. One day, she was late picking me up and, to her utter amazement, found me sitting there, surrounded by a small group of other kids, listening intently to my words.

'She was telling them a story, Ging,' said Molly proudly when my dad came home. 'I'm sure she's going to do something big. Maybe she'll go on the stage.'

Oh dear. Such was my mum's conviction that I was heading for superstardom, she insisted my dad also fork out for dancing classes for me, though I had no real physical aptitude for dance, just an incessant desire to show off, to throw myself around and pose.

Once a week, we'd trot round the corner to a basement on the Kingsland Road. The dance studio was called Miss Betty's, and for two shillings a session 'Miss Betty', a dark-haired former twenties chorus girl turning to seed, would plonk away on the piano and bark out instructions to her tiny pupils. The classes were very small, just four or five kids. Sometimes it was just me. Which isn't surprising: we were in Bash Street Kids territory, not posh Richmond or Roehampton.

'Bra-bra, gateway – up to the skies,' she'd instruct the little Dalston wanabee Markovas like myself as we struggled to move our arms and legs to copy her. (These odd phrases were descriptions of the shapes we were meant to be making with our arms.) Alas, I never had the makings of any sort of ballerina, though I loved the pink satin shoes with their blocked toes that my mum bought me specially from Freed in Covent Garden. Standing 'en pointe' was a buzz – if you could manage to stand on your toes for more than thirty seconds, that is, which I couldn't. My tap-dancing skills – jump, shuffle, jump, shuffle, toe-heel, toe-heel in my little black shoes with metal toe pieces – weren't much to write home about either. Yet I was OK at singing, mainly because I could remember all the words perfectly and just about follow a tune. So by the time I was heading for primary school, such was my mum's conviction that fame and fortune lay ahead that I'd started to believe in my own hype. If someone keeps telling you and everyone else how wonderful you are, your self-belief soars. And so singing, dancing, reciting and performing became a big part of my life, along with reading, until I was close to my teens. And so did a certain sort of self-confidence, the confidence of the overindulged…

However, this over-eagerness to perform and mouth-off got me into trouble when I was about four years old.

It is summer and we are at the seaside, on our annual holiday at Cliftonville on the Kent Coast. I am wearing a pink ruched swimsuit, a stripey taffeta bow holds up my unruly mop. Molly and I are in an outdoor pavilion, in the audience, watching other holidaymakers, mostly kids, take to the stage. They are supposed to be performing, strutting their stuff for their mums and dads, but, as is sometimes the way with small children, most find themselves tongue-tied and reluctant when actually faced with an audience. One boy is hauled onto the stage, bursts into tears and has to be quickly yanked off.

'I can do better than that!' I declare, bored and fidgety as usual when confronted with a situation where nothing much seems to be happening. Everyone, every holidaymaker, parent and kid, focuses on me and my mum. And the MC, beret on his head, mike in his hand, figures he'll use this and teach the little brat a lesson into the bargain. It might get a few laughs. In his line of business, you have to work with what you get.

'OK, if you can do better, come up here and show us,' he says, fed up with his day job, coaxing free entertainment out of noisy holidaymaking Londoners.

Molly looks at me nervously, wanting to rescue me from my Big Mistake. I've opened my trap and set myself up good and proper.

But I don't shrink back or cling to my mum, for some reason. Nor do I cry. The desire to get up there and show off, despite the unexpected summons, is now powerful in me.

So my mum guides me to the side of the wooden stage where someone lifts me onto it.

'So what's your name, then?' says the MC.

'And what are you going to sing for us today that's better than that?'

Everyone laughs at the tiny tot with the inflated ego.

'My name is Jakerlin,' I tell him seriously, unsure of my ground now I'm faced with the awesome reality of an audience somewhat bigger than I'm used to at home. 'Don' wanna sing a song, wanna say a poem,' I say, somewhat defiantly.

'OK Jakerlin,' he sighs. Another ripple of laughter goes through the watching crowd. A photographer takes a snap of the tot who thought she could do better. I still have it.

And I get through the four-verse poem, called An Old Rat's Tale. 'He was a rat and she was a rat and down in one hole they did dwell...' I make a pretty poor fist of it, frequently pausing to remember lines, and get more laughs than claps when I finish. My mum doesn't know whether to be proud or embarrassed for me when she yanks me off the stage. But I know I've blown it, one of the first times in my life that I begin to realise I should have kept my big mouth firmly shut – and stayed on the safe side.

Did someone say that lessons like this teach you how to control your emotions, measure your reaction, think a bit before verbalising your feelings? I'd like to tell you that this little seaside episode taught me a valuable lesson. But I won't lie. It was only the beginning of a life spent all too frequently regretting my over-enthusiasm to say exactly what I think, the minute I think it. You do improve a bit with age, of course. But I still blame the parents.

They never knew when it was time to tell their little darling to sit down and shut up.

CHAPTER 11
A PIANO

We are in a big white house, somewhere in a place called Surrey.

I have never been inside a house like this, so I am entranced, if somewhat awed, by everything around me: the thick, plush, pale carpets, tall vases on polished surfaces containing huge colourful blooms, exquisite antique chairs with silk cushions, elegant long windows with velvet drapes overlooking an immense garden that seems to go on for ever... such a plush, quiet, different world from the one we inhabit.

We've been driven here in a very big chauffeur driven car, my mum and I, all the way from home to meet our host, Lol, a good friend of my dad's from the pub. Lol and his wife Maggie have invited us here for high tea. My dad, of course, is working. He's been pally with this couple for ages, sometimes going to West-End shows with them. Lol and Maggie, who don't have any kids of their own, have insisted we come over. They want to meet me – and show us their lovely home.

Lol, a very handsome man in his forties, with slicked-back dark brown hair, and a look of Robert Taylor, a movie favourite of the fifties, had been a publican before the war. Now, we don't know what he does. Or rather, no one is saying. But this big house, with its own driveway, seems to confirm what my mum has always told me about Lol and Maggie. Whenever they're mentioned, she says, 'They're very rich. He owns a Bentley, that's one of the most expensive cars you can buy. And she gets all her clothes from abroad, can you believe that? She had this beautiful white organdie blouse on; I had to ask her where it came from. "I think it's from Paris," she said, like she'd just picked it up off a stall in the Lane!'

For my mum, clothes were everything, the signal to the world that gave you all the status – and admiration – you needed. By now, my dad's ever-open wallet meant her own crammed wardrobe bore witness to this: an array of crepe de Chine dresses, made to measure, neat two-piece tailored suits, coats in fine wools, skirts of every variety, blouses made of silk and satins: she had no need to envy anyone, really, when it came to looking good. Nowadays, she'd be buying up bigtime at Selfridges, Sloane Street or online at Net-a-Porter. But there's nothing remotely new about female one- upmanship when it comes to what you wear: Maggie, by my mum's glamour-girl standards, could shop in Paris – ergo Maggie Had It All.

Most of my dad's friends were atypical East Enders, rough and ready Jewish stallholders or cockney shopkeepers with a ribald sense of humour, wisecracking their way through life; the sort of people who loved a laugh, a knees-up. Yet Lol and

Maggie stood apart from the rest – rich, mysterious, almost exotic in a way, and everything about them smacked of English gentility. They had class.

Lol, this particular day, is immaculate, expensive shoes shined to perfection, perfectly cut Savile Row suit and discreet silk tie. He shows us around their vast palace. My mum, for once, is subdued, quiet as we climb the soft-carpeted stairs and Lol reveals the upstairs area. Four bedrooms, two big bathrooms, all beautifully furnished, everything perfect. There's even a library with more books than I've ever seen in one place. And there are lots of photos in big silver frames, mostly of Maggie and Lol on holiday in faraway places like the South of France. She's a stunning redhead, manicured, perfectly coiffed, discreetly bejewelled, reed thin.

'Where's Maggie?' Mum ventures. 'Oh she's gone out in her car,' says Lol airily. 'She had an appointment in the West End. She's sorry she'll miss you. But there'll be another time.'

This is extremely odd. Maggie was reportedly dying to meet me. And why hasn't Lol said a word about her mysterious vanishing act until my mum actually asked him?

Our tour over, he suggests I wander round their garden. 'Go and have a look at the flowers, Jacky,' he says, opening the big French doors and ushering me outside.

I'm a bit bemused by all this grandeur and space, but nonetheless I step outside and wander around for a bit, amidst the manicured lawns and the pretty flowerbeds. But it's all too much for me, a true Hackney kid whose daily vistas are grungy crowded streets and shops and street markets, with the occasional trip to the seaside or the West End thrown in. I don't really know – or yet appreciate – vast green spaces: I've only been in a big garden a couple of times before on a rare visit to my Sussex cousins. So the huge garden, for me, is somehow strange, intimidating, rather than a delight. I walk around for a while. Then I step back through the French doors. My mum rushes forward and takes my hand. 'Let's see what Lol's got for us for tea, Jac.'

Lol is the perfect host. In a big dining room, at a long table covered by a white linen cloth, everything is already set up for our tea: tiny triangular egg-and-cress sandwiches, sliced fruitcake, warm, freshly baked scones, clotted cream, raspberry jam, butter, linen napkins, silver cutlery, fine porcelain crockery. He pours out our tea and encourages me to tuck into the scones (not that I need much encouragement). We spend a happy half hour, Lol putting us both at ease, asking me about dancing class, what books I like, talking to Molly about shows they've seen, a genial, utterly charming, urbane man in a sophisticated setting. I'm not used to it but I'm pretty impressed. So is my mum, although she's a bit subdued.

In the corner of the big room stands a large black piano. I can't play but Lol encourages me to muck around on the keys for a bit, while he and Molly finish their tea. Once they've finished, he walks over to the piano and seats himself on the piano stool.

'Now I'm going to play something for you two,' he says, winking at me.

Then he starts to play, a skilful, experienced pianist, his fingers barely seem to touch the keys. He starts singing too, a song that is very popular at the time; everyone knows it. It's the theme song from a movie called *Moulin Rouge*, which was a big hit in 1952. We haven't seen the movie, but we know the song. It's a lovely song, a plaintive lover's plea called 'Where is Your Heart?'.

'Whenever we kiss, I worry and wonder, your lips may be near. But where is your heart?' sings Lol, his voice well modulated and smooth, hitting the notes perfectly. Molly and I are entranced, mesmerised by it all. At one point, my mother takes out a hankie and dabs her eyes. This handsome man, singing this plaintive song for us in such a beautiful setting: it's a moment to remember. But my childish antennae can sense a certain poignancy in his voice; it's all tinged with sadness, though I couldn't have told you why.

Half an hour later, Lol says farewell to us as we climb into the big Bentley and his chauffeur silently drives us home, through winding green country lanes of even bigger, grander houses than the one we've just left.

'Why did he sing us that sad song, mum?' I ask Molly, who seems lost in some kind of wistful reverie.

'And where was Maggie? I thought she wanted to meet me.'

'So did I Jac,' sighs Molly. 'I don't know about the singing. But it's a lovely song, isn't it?'

I don't hear any more about Lol and Maggie for ages. Neither of my parents mention them. Then, some months later, I ask my mum about them: I can't quite forget the handsome man at the piano and the haunting love song.

'Look, Jac, we don't know what happened but…Maggie's dead. Ging says she was at home, asleep in bed. They think she had some sort of heart attack in the night. Lol's so upset; he's sold the house and moved to America. He's got some kind of business there.'

By now, I'm such an inquisitive kid that I'm not at all satisfied with this.

I'm shocked that she's dead, of course, but there are so many overhanging questions from our brief visit. Why didn't Maggie stick around to see us that day? And why was Lol singing that sad song? Something was very wrong. But I couldn't put my finger on what it was.

Yet there were, of course, rumours swirling around the Lane and the pub. And when I ask my mum again, a few weeks later, she tells me what people are saying. It's pretty nasty, but she tells me just the same (she knows all too well that at nine, I won't let up with my 'Why this? Why that?' questions until I get a satisfactory answer).

'They're saying that he bumped her off and got away with it. They weren't getting on apparently. There's a story that he had another woman set up in a flat in the West End. I dunno. I don't believe all that stuff about him doing it. She died, that's all. They all sit around in the George & Dragon and make things up, if you ask me.'

Yet I never quite forgot that afternoon tea in the big house in Surrey – and the bad news that came afterwards. And, incredibly, decades later, when my mum is in her eighties, long widowed and living alone, we start to reminisce one day about those years of my childhood and I mention the story of Lol and Maggie.

Yes, she remembers it.

'They said he bumped her off, didn't they?' she muses. 'Hmm...well you never knew then, with some of your dad's friends, what they might get up to.

'But he was a real ladies man. He tried it on with me, in

the house, when you were out in the garden. He tried to kiss me – with you around too! I was so embarrassed. And then you came back in! But I never told your father, he'd have gone potty.'

I'm not surprised Lol fancied my mum; many did. But the spicy revelation still doesn't solve the mystery of it all. Yet to this day, if I ever hear that song, an icy shiver runs down my spine. Where indeed, was Lol's heart? And what was the truth about Maggie?

CHAPTER 12
FARTHINGS

I hated farthings. Coins mean so little now. But they were a big deal to kids back then. You could take the 'empties', empty glass bottles of pop, like Corona fizzy lemonade or Tizer (fizzy, red and known as 'the Appetiser', a testament to the power of advertising), back to the local off-licence or sweet shop and exchange them for tuppence each. Even now, the ancient pounds, shilling and pence currency, replaced by decimal currency in 1971, carries a potent nostalgia factor. Brass threepenny bits were the most attractive coins to kids, heavier than pennies and they actually bought you an ounce or two of your favourite sweets, neatly served up in a paper bag. Every kid liked threepenny bits. You had spending power.

But farthings were something else, piffling and irrelevant. You couldn't buy anything for a farthing with its daft little wren on the front, though they didn't actually stop being legal tender until 1960. Because they were so titchy, they had a habit of slipping down the sides of sofas or remaining hidden under floorboards for years. So if no one was around, one of my favourite kiddie joys was to chuck a handful of farthings out, right over the top of the landing outside our flat.

It has to be said, throwing money around for no reason was a bit of a metaphor for the backdrop to my childhood – using money to buy whatever you fancied, never treating it with any respect, blithely assuming there'd be more whenever you needed it. Live for the moment. Tomorrow never comes. All the clichés of careless living. And, essentially, a very 'street' way of viewing money, if you ran a busy market stall, traded in black-market goods or took bets in pubs like my father. You could always go out and earn more, even if the method wasn't strictly legit. And once earned again it was there to spend. Or, in the case of some of my dad's punters, there to deprive the wife and kids of any extra by putting it on an each-way bet on the 3 o'clock at Redcar. And losing.

I never had a piggy bank, nor did I ever receive any encouragement to save money. 'Saving' was a meaningless word, never heard or discussed at home. After I reached about five, I'd be given the odd sixpence or shilling to spend by myself, frequently in one of the two sweet shops close by. The smaller shop, bang on the corner of our street on Shacklewell Lane, was my favourite: row after row of big glass jars containing aniseed balls, sherbet lemons, gobstoppers, chewy Black Jacks or Fruit Salads. Or there was a delight called a sherbet fizz, white sherbet in a yellow cardboard tube with a liquorice stick to suck out the sherbet. It usually got very messy because the liquorice would go all soggy. But the fizzy sherbet was a real buzz. Or you could get four Black Jacks (aniseed-flavoured black squares) for a penny that kept you chewing for ages. But if any kid tried to buy 'just one Black

Jack' with a farthing, the request was usually greeted with a shake of the head. Everyone knew farthings were unacceptable – but of course, kids would try, just the same, if that was all they had.

Despite rationing, sweet shops were as ubiquitous then as high-street mobile phone stores are now; the biggest and the best was on Kingsland Road, next door to the ABC cinema and opposite the 649 bus stop. It did a roaring trade once rationing restrictions ended. Amazingly, the site of the other nearest sweet shop on the opposite side of Shacklewell Lane remains there to this day, a newsagents and corner store nowadays surrounded by what were then big factory buildings, and now converted into trendy flats.

It was a very big day in my sugarlustful world, when sweet rationing formally ended in 1953, the year the Queen got to wear her crown in public for the first time: as a reward for helping keep her in business, we kids got as many sweets as we could afford.

It was a cold, wet February morning, yet I virtually dragged my mum down the Kingsland Road, past the market to a sweet shop next door to Sainsbury's where, rumour had it, you could actually buy as many Crunchie bars as you wanted. But alas, the word had already spread through the streets of Dalston and beyond. By the time we got there, their stock of Crunchies had nigh on vanished. But even so, when we left, me triumphantly clutching the last two Crunchies in their purple wrappers, one in each little gloved hand, it was a memorable moment. Even if, for a greedy little chocoholic, two could never be enough: did I mention that one of the first baby words I uttered was 'choc-a-choc'?

By then, at around age 9, I was developing an avid reading habit, so the bulk of my ever-increasing pocket money, now half a crown (or two shillings and sixpence), usually had a focus beyond the sweet shop: buying books and magazines from the shops on Kingsland Road. Initially, the glossy picture books with Royals were top of my list, later came the weekly delight of magazines like *School Friend*. (The Silent Three were a favourite, three boarding-school girls who wore robes and hoods – early hoodies? – and went round the place doing good deeds anonymously.) Then later I developed the *Photoplay* movie mag habit.

At the same time, when it became apparent I had such a hunger for books, my mum steered me in the direction of our two local libraries, one in Dalston Lane (small, but nearly always had an Enid Blyton I hadn't yet discovered like *Mallory Towers* or *The Famous Five*) and a less-frequented one a bit further away in Farleigh Road, Stoke Newington. Jean Plaidy, who wrote many historical novels, became another big favourite. I devoured her books.

Yet there was another free library for me at home too: my dad was a voracious reader in those early post-war years, a regular *Daily Mirror* buyer and a consumer of London's three evening papers of the time. 'Star, News and Standard!' was a familiar sound then on every London street corner; Ginger would often come home and chuck all three on the sofa, keeping his work-related newspaper, *Sporting Life*, folded up in his overcoat pocket.

My parents' bedroom boasted a small, cheap wooden bookcase with a collection of paperbacks about the war, hardbacks too from authors like Somerset Maugham (*Liza of*

Lambeth) H.E. Bates (*Fair Stood the Wind for France*) Edmund Wilson's *Memoirs of Hecate County* (a naughty one which I flicked through, but didn't really understand at that age) and Nevil Shute (*A Town Like Alice*). I didn't read them all, of course, but later, the slightly more salacious ones like *My Wicked, Wicked Ways*, an autobiography by movie star Errol Flynn written just before he died, were devoured. The one thing my childhood didn't lack was access to reading material.

On Sunday visits to my grandparents, I eventually found a way out of the boredom of trying to make conversation with Anthony by immersing myself in some very ancient copies of the *Illustrated London News*, a magazine which had been first published in the mid-1800s and copies of which my grandparents had obviously hung onto for decades.

There were no outdoor activities to speak of. Physical endeavour of any kind was not my forte; I was a bookish, indoor kid. Anyway, there was nowhere to play. The street wasn't fit to act as any kind of playground, though at primary school we'd play the traditional, fun playground games like hopscotch (I never got to play Kiss Chase, alas, because I was at an all-girls' primary), and later on I learned the rudiments of swimming at the local baths.

Unfortunately, I never learned properly. I was towed along on a rope by the teacher, splashing away merrily, but I never got beyond that stage which was a pity: on seaside jaunts, my dad, who loved sport, especially football, relished his annual bout of swimming. My mum would cheerfully pose for the camera standing in the water in a beautiful white bathing suit – complete with big earrings and watch – yet she never ventured further out to get wet or spoil her hairdo. Even the dancing lessons at Miss Betty's were merely a part of the reciting/singing/showing off bit: I was never going to be a proper dancer.

I was very much a loner. An only child learns a degree of self-sufficiency, of course, as a survival tactic, yet there weren't many other children in my early world. At school, I didn't start to really form out-of-school friendships with other girls until I was about ten: I was far too preoccupied with reading, writing, getting good marks and going to my dancing classes. The only other child of around my age I was more or less thrown together with on seaside holidays and regular visits to the Lane was Anthony, whose parents initially lived in the Lane so he lived through far more of our grandparents' world than I. But there wasn't much to draw us together; many years later Anthony revealed to my mother that as a timid, shy child he was quite scared of me. 'Sometimes she'd kick or pinch me when no one was looking,' was his recall of our relationship. Oh dear.

Most of the time, it was just me and my mum. Imperceptibly, as I grew up, I absorbed many of her preoccupations: clothes, hairdos, make-up. And I also demonstrated scant interest in the things she wasn't especially bothered with, like domesticity. Of course she cooked all the time – there were no ready meals or takeaways then, other than fish-and-chip shops in Kingsland Road, or jellied eels from Tubby Isaacs in the Lane or Cooks Pie Shop near Ridley Road, things we rarely indulged in – but to Molly, cooking was a chore, a duty, something you had to do. She was reasonably competent: there were never burnt or tasteless meals. But I never learned to cook. The kitchen was tiny, certainly. But she didn't offer – and I never asked. As for cleaning, washing clothes, ironing, even making beds or washing up, my mum never enlisted me to get stuck in, learn all about being a housewife or homemaker. I had a very cushy deal.

Years later, my dad would commandeer the pokey kitchen to cook his beloved bacon-and-egg breakfasts, neatly laying out the strips of bacon, tomato slices and sausages on plates well in advance, ready for the big fry-up, an obsessive Saturday morning pre-Spurs football ground ritual that developed when his life had taken a different turn. And at one stage, Molly did show me how to thread and wield a sewing needle to create a neat seam or sew on a button. But there was no attempt at teaching me the rudiments of chopping, stirring, baking or frying as I grew up. All I ever did was occasionally shell peas.

Eating out wasn't an everyday part of ordinary family life in the fifties: the highlight of an outing to the high street or to the West End with my mother might be a trip to a Lyons Corner House, the only decent chain of eating places that existed back then. You could get a cup of tea, a salad or a roll and butter – or a proper meal, depending on the time of day. What thrilled me about any Corner House outing was the chance to dive into a Knickerbocker Glory, a fabulous gooey confection of tinned fruit, jelly, cream and ice cream piled high in a tall glass. Bliss.

Things changed in the mid-fifties when the Lyons Corner House in Coventry Street, Piccadilly, introduced an exciting new addition to the menu, the Wimpy, Britain's first post-war attempt at a burger. It tasted gorgeous, a combo of fat, salt and ground beef topped with a big dollop of ketchup from the red squeezy bottle on each table. Very soon, even Kingsland High Street sported its first Wimpy Bar as they started to spring up, Starbucks' style, across the land, gradually changing our eating habits. The birth of fast-food culture as we now know it.

CHAPTER 13
A WEDDING

My dad was a genuine, 100 per cent cockney, born within the sound of Bow Bells in Whitechapel – and incredibly proud of it all his life. Part of that sense of pride came, I believe, from rubbing shoulders with all sorts of Londoners other than the Petticoat Lane locals: the posh City gents, the coppers, the well-heeled publicans, the bank managers and the journalists he drank with frequently in the pub: this kind of camaraderie linked everyone living and working around the City area (what we now call the Square Mile) itself, with its long trading history and traditions. My grandfather also took pride in his status as a true Londoner – his family had been running businesses in and around the Lane for well over a century.

My mum, born in posh Kensington, with an aspiring Russian immigrant father, had had a much more genteel upbringing where the emphasis was on culture, music and art; as a tot she'd learned the violin and while she was not remotely bookish, many of her siblings were artistic and

creative. So she wasn't over-familiar with East End culture –
pubs, rowdy knees-ups, that sort of thing – till my dad started
courting her.

Nonetheless, the cultural divide didn't stop her from
spending ages planning her outfits and getting dolled up to the
nines for the big 'dos', mostly weddings, my dad's friends and
family went in for in the early fifties. I sported a frilly organdie
bridesmaid's outfit and a posy for a few of these – still showing
the signs of a big bout of mumps on one occasion – and these
mostly Jewish weddings would be pretty lavish affairs with
hundreds of guests, live music, cash wedding gifts – and as
much as anyone could eat in one sitting.

In the early fifties, my dad's brother, Neville, courted and
married a girl almost half his age – Neville was thirty five,
Barb was extremely pretty and nineteen (he'd told her he was
thirty and she believed him, only discovering the truth after
nearly four decades of marriage when she saw his death
certificate).

Neville's wedding was a huge bash, paid for by Barb's family
and held at a north London hotel. 350 people sat down to a
sumptuous five-course meal, followed by dancing to a live big
band.

Jewish wedding receptions, by tradition, though often quite
extravagant, are not, generally speaking, an excuse for
everyone to get well and truly drunk. Alcohol, of course, is
available, but most people tend to have one or two drinks, the
odd glass of wine and no more.

So on hearing that his son's wedding was in the planning
process The Old Man had a major concern. A few of his big-
betting punters were, of course, on the guest list. And they

liked Scotch, especially Johnny Walker Black Label. This, of course, was both expensive and not readily available in the austerity days.

'I'm definitely not paying for the Black Label,' said Mary, the bride's mother, a woman renowned for her iron will – and open dislike of alcohol and public houses.

'Nah, I'll provide the Black Label for the reception,' said the Old Man obligingly. And so, courtesy of the black market and his group of 'anything, anytime' contacts, the Black Label bottles were sourced for the wedding reception, costing him a sizeable wad of crinkly fivers. He then generously suggested using his contacts to get Barb a really fantastic engagement ring at a very good price. And indeed, once procured, the ring was a superb sparkler; Barb loved the big diamond as she proudly showed it off to her girlfriends.

But once valued, months after the honeymoon, she discovered the truth: the ring was worthless, a paste fake (yet another typical Petticoat Lane con trick of the times, passing off worthless jewellery for wads of cash). Of course, neither she nor her new hubby dared say a word to The Old Man.

At the wedding, The Old Man, his punters and Ginger emptied the Black Label bottles with alacrity. For some reason, no matter what he drank, The Old Man never showed obvious signs of drunkenness: you never saw him actually fool around or get lairy, though we all knew that in private he could be very stroppy. And the punters and their wives, somewhat garishly costumed, like most of the female guests, in long beaded satin dresses and fox-fur stoles, thoroughly enjoyed themselves, the men holding their drink well.

But not Ginger, alas.

I am seated at a children's table in my frilly bridesmaid's dress with all the other kids. We are just finishing off our ice cream and fruit salad when it happens. My parents are with a group of relatives at a nearby table. And my dad, well-oiled by now, decides to serenade his brother, the blushing bride and the assembled guests. So he climbs onto his chair and spontaneously bursts into loud – and very pissed – song.

'AALL of me….why not take AAALL of me, cantcha see, I'm no good wivvaaht ya,' he croons, well out of tune. I am instantly uncomfortable, trapped with this embarrassing evidence of my dad's unruly behaviour. I squirm in my seat and avoid the eyes of the other kids. A few older kids are giggling and nudging each other, they've seen it before at dos like this. The bride's family, on the top table, are stony faced, clearly not at all impressed. Even the band doesn't dare tune in and back him.

This outburst, of course, confirms what Barb's family, respectable and comfortably off, have already suspected about Neville and his family: they are a rowdy mob of Petticoat Lane ne'er-do-wells. They may be flush with cash – The Old Man's largesse with the Black Label had been anticipated, even if still frowned upon. But their Barb has definitely Married Down. (It's a good job that at that point, they didn't know about the worthless sparkler.)

OK, it's a wedding with the usual jokey speeches and noisy toasts. And later, when the dancing gets going, the guests will all take to the floor to link arms for the usual raucous versions of the Hokey Cokey and Knees Up Mother Brown. It's a far from subdued gathering. But this solo, very pissed person's version of 'All of Me' is definitely not relevant to the occasion.

It's way out of order: you just don't do this sort of thing at this kind of bash. But as I sit there silently praying he'll finish, longing to get up and run away, wishing it wasn't my dad who was making all the noise and making people tut and titter, I look over at my mum. Isn't she upset?

But no. Molly's fine. She's smiling. Noisy, loud, raucous and embarrassing as my dad is, it just doesn't seem to bother her. As Ginger finishes his wailing and attempts to step down from the chair, he stumbles and falls over. Oh no. More shame, more embarrassment, though by now people are ignoring the whole thing, talking and laughing as if it hasn't happened. Unsteadily he picks himself up. 'OK, Mol,' he winks at his spouse, practically falling into his chair, reaching for another glass. Mol just leans back, gives him a half smile and a reassuring pat on the shoulder – and carries on chatting to the person next to her.

This kind of behaviour, boozing until you fell flat on your

face, was somewhat at odds with the perceived behaviour of Jewish people: Jews aren't exactly renowned for their love of heavy drinking or pubs. But the Lane, though very much a Jewish enclave then, was also a bit of a cultural potpourri. It wasn't like the somewhat posher suburbs where everyone behaved according to type. In the Lane, you earned money however you could, regardless of traditional stereotypes. So there were pubs around the Lane that were run by Jewish families who'd been there for decades. And gambling, of course, brings in all comers, all backgrounds: so keeping punters happy with Black Label or whatever else they wanted to drink was far more important to my dad and grandfather than worrying about observing certain social norms.

Hackney and the adjoining areas of Stoke Newington and Stamford Hill were, back then, heavily populated by Jewish families – though the drift away of upwardly mobile, more successful Jewish families to the smarter areas of north-west London and the outer suburbs had already started back in the thirties. So while we lived very much in a Jewish milieu, my dad wasn't interested or involved enough in Jewish culture itself to follow any traditions.

Not long after he'd returned from India, my mum laid the table for dinner one Friday night, setting out the traditional Jewish Sabbath candles on the dining table. When Ginger came in from work, she lit them, something she'd learned at home, as a child. While it had not been possible to observe this ritual regularly through the chaos of wartime, this was one thing which, to her, spoke of normality – and family tradition.

Ginger was having none of it. 'We won't have any of that,'

he snapped, dousing the candles and removing the candlesticks from the table.

'Ging, I thought it'd be nice,' said my mum, knowing already that her case was hopeless.

'No, not in this house,' was the response.

So I grew up in a home where being Jewish was a fact of life, living our lives around other Jews. But it more or less stopped there. I never learned Hebrew, went to a synagogue or celebrated any Jewish festivals in the traditional way. Nor was there any pressure to learn more about the customs, what they meant. And my mum, despite growing up in a Jewish family where the customs had been observed, didn't seem to really mind the absence of these traditions. She cooked certain kinds of Jewish food, like lokshen soup (chicken-and-noodle soup) and chopped liver, because she knew how to – and my dad liked eating them. But he also liked eating the things Jewish people weren't supposed to eat: bacon, eggs, pork sausages, that sort of thing. That was how he'd grown up.

Talk about mixed messages. Now, of course, I know that there are many non- practising Jews all over the world; we weren't that unusual. Yet, like most children, I shrank in fear and embarrassment from my dad's drinking because it made him 'different'; I didn't see other people's dads getting drunk and making a mess of themselves. Later, of course, I understood that anyone, from any background, can be an alcoholic, junkie, adulterer, crook, you name it, they're human beings with frailties, the same as everyone else. But back then, my dad's heavy drinking in the midst of a seemingly non-drinking Jewish environment created a somewhat confusing situation for me.

For instance, I became a bit of a swot at my girls' primary school, Princess May on Kingsland High Street, and didn't like the idea of missing a single lesson. So the first time the big annual Jewish holiday came round, Yom Kippur, the Day of Atonement (the day when all Jews must fast and cease all normal activity for twenty-four hours), and it coincided with a school day, I rebelled. I didn't want to take a whole day off from school. Yet it was one day my dad did take off from work, probably because many of his punters were Jewish and subsequently, most of the East End betting fraternity did, once a year, observe their cultural heritage. So he insisted I stay home.

'She's gotta stay home, it's the Black Fast,' he told Molly. (I never did find out why he used this phrase, nor did I ever hear anyone else use it.)

But I too insisted, stamping my tiny foot, doing my 'Wanna go' number. And, as usual, they gave in.

When my class teacher, Miss Hallinan, a kindly Irish woman, saw me walk in that day she stood there, aghast. What was going on? There weren't that many Jewish kids at my primary school, but she was familiar with the Jewish customs – and the one day when all Jewish life in the area ground to a standstill.

'Just what are you doing here, Jacqueline Hyams?'

'Mum and dad said it was all right,' I said, defiantly, though already unsure of my ground. 'And miss, I don't want to miss classes,' I added plaintively.

But she wouldn't have it. I had to go home. Now. She even marched me across the main road outside the school. Miserably, I made my way back down Arcola Street, stomping up the stairs to our flat. My dad, of course, was vindicated when he opened the door and I ran into my bedroom.

'See…that teacher knows what she's doing,' he told my mum later.

But all it did was create even more confusion. To me, it didn't make sense. Why should I take a day off school, missing out on learning, for something we didn't really bother with? Why did this one day make any difference?

I never got any coherent answers. They were, in their way, trying to instil a sense of the importance of Jewish culture in me. Yet it was too random and indirect for it to make an impact.

A few years later, approaching my teens, I had a memorable conversation with my dad about being Jewish. I'd seen the books by his bed about the war – and what had happened to millions of Jews in the Holocaust and the concentration camps. No kid could ever forget the message of those terrible photos taken in the camps when the Allies marched in. I knew all about the gassings, the prejudice and the ongoing persecution of the Jewish people. Fascists like Mosley were still very active in the East End after the war, so I knew full well that people disliked, even hated us as Jews, simply because we existed.

'Your best bet is to stick with Jewish people,' Ginger warned me.

'That way you'll be safe, because you never know if – and when – the non-Jews might do the dirty on you.'

'But…you're friends with lots of people who aren't Jewish, dad,' I pointed out. 'Look at Len from the café and his family, they're not Jewish and they're your friends. And Charlie Riley, you're always out with him.'

'That's different,' Ginger said. 'I grew up with them, it doesn't count.'

Huh? I pondered all this later; I didn't want to ask my mum because I suspected she'd follow the same unsatisfactory line. And I came to the conclusion that somehow, the logic of this was wrong, off the wall.

Jews were a minority, a small group of people. Fine. Yet it didn't make sense to me to stick fast to just that one small group. The world was made up of millions and millions of people. Maybe some hated your guts, wanted you dead; but they couldn't ALL be out to do you harm. Terrible things had happened to us, yes. But that was the past – and instinctively, I sensed that I didn't want to be locked in thrall to the past in that way. It could hold you back.

Essentially, I decided there and then that I didn't want to limit my life to just one small group of people and avoid the rest out of fear, just to feel safe. The world was big – and I already knew I wanted to be out there, in the midst of it all, finding out about everything. If being Jewish was going to stop me from making my own choices in life, then I wasn't having any of it. I never openly voiced this view, understanding all too well that it wouldn't be well received. But for me the decision stuck fast.

You could say I rejected my dad's somewhat restrictive view of our background because I had an overwhelming curiosity about life. Or you could say I was just an independent thinker. Take your pick…

CHAPTER 14
SCHOOL MILK

If there was one thing about being a post-war child that was virtually guaranteed to put you off milk for life, it was the free bottled milk we were given at school. It was vile, pale, watery, insipid stuff. On a bad day, you'd get one with a horrible creepy skin that had formed over the top; truly disgusting. Fridges didn't arrive in ordinary homes until the mid-fifties, which didn't help: in winter, the small glass bottles would be left to warm up on the radiators, making it taste even more horrible. And if you demurred, all you'd hear was 'drink it up, it's good for you'. OK, it was a good idea for the post-war authorities to boost the nation's nutrition by providing free milk in the classroom. Many kids needed all the help they could get. But like many of the well-meaning intentions of the government, it had a drawback: it was virtually undrinkable. In my case it was the start of a personal lifelong revulsion against all things milk. As soon as I could, I stopped drinking it. Ever. Even now, if someone mistakenly stirs my coffee with a milky spoon, it goes straight in the sink.

What I did like was the free bottled concentrated orange juice, made available by the NHS to boost kids' Vitamin C levels. It came in a glass bottle with a blue screw cap and it was pure delight whenever I spotted a new one in the pantry. I wasn't so keen on another free dietary supplement, cod-liver oil, which you'd sup, with a shudder, by the spoonful. But I was quite keen on Virol, a dark malt extract with Vitamin A, which came in a big metal tin. This was sweet and thick, the general idea to give kids more bulk. And luckily, perhaps because I always saw my dad drink a lot of it – he always had a big jug by his bedside – I developed a lifetime tap water drinking habit. It beats drinking milk any day.

My dad had grown up in a household where typically English food was a Very Big deal – especially things like the Sunday roast. My mother's culinary upbringing had been the direct opposite: a bit of a health freak, even in those days, my grandfather Oliver had insisted that their family ate lots of fruit and vegetables and very little meat or chicken. Unsweetened yogurt each day was also one of Oliver's favourites.

Yet despite this gulf in their tastes, my mum cheerfully adapted to cooking all the food that came through the front door, via Wag's black-market deliveries: the big joints of beef, legs of lamb, the fresh salmon, plaice and halibut from Petticoat Lane, usually fried by my mum in big batches, making the tiny cramped kitchen reek for hours. My dad was consistently puffed up about the fact that we were eating so well, while others struggled or got poorer quality food.

'It's the best stuff that only goes to the big hotels,' he'd inform us proudly, time and time again. I grew up hearing him constantly informing us that he provided 'the finest and the best' for our table, just in case we didn't realise were lucky sods to have so much wonderful food. Alas, it was all lost on me, a skinny kid who'd rather be scoffing sweets, or eating my way through a bag of broken Smith's crisps (even crisps were a luxury item before rationing ended; the only variety available were the bags of broken ones which were 'seconds' that appeared in the shops occasionally).

As for my mum, she appreciated our good fortune – but only up to a point. Had we just relied, like most people, on rations and the odd bit of 'extra' from behind the butcher's counter, she'd have been just as happy.

We are at my grandparents' flat in Stoney Lane. It's a big family gathering, a late Sunday lunch. Two of my dad's siblings are sitting with us at the dining table, his younger sister Doris, brother George and their respective partners. The Old Man, in shirtsleeves and braces at the head of the table, is poised to carve the enormous roast chicken that lies, glistening and aromatic, stuffed with Paxo, before him, ready to be devoured by his family.

Each plate is proffered up to The Old Man who expertly carves huge portions for all. Lips are already smacking, as my grandmother passes round the gravy, the big plates of roast potatoes, parsnips, carrots, peas, onions, stuffing and green pickled cucumbers. Sloppy as usual, I manage to get hot gravy all down my new dress. Molly is furiously dabbing at the dress with her hankie when suddenly, out of the blue, my Aunt Doris flings her knife and fork down on the table. And then she starts crying her eyes out. It's a sorry sight. Pretty, fair-haired and usually quite passive, this is a Doris I've never seen before.

'It's not fair!' she screeches between huge heaving sobs. 'It's always the same!'

Then she gets up and runs out of the dining room, heading for the outside loo on the landing.

Everything goes silent. You can hear the big black clock on the wall ticking it's so quiet. And, of course, in that typically English way when they're embarrassed, everyone sitting there pretends the outburst hasn't happened. No reaction. All eyes down. Focused on the Sunday roast. There's the discreet clatter of cutlery on plates. But no one is saying anything.

'Mm…the skin's really nice and crispy,' Molly ventures, hoping to break the silence. My dad looks at her as if to say, 'shut the fuck up'; even he is keeping schtoom. The Old Man grunts appreciatively but remains impassive behind his big black specs, chomping away relentlessly. Miriam wears her normal face: unsmiling, browned off with her lot, toying with the food on her plate. I am puzzled. Why is my aunt crying so much she has to run away? Is she ill? We're almost finished when Doris returns to the table and, as if nothing has happened, attacks her plate, though her face is downcast. Nothing more is said. And once the meal is finished, everyone is keen to scatter: my mum quickly buttons up my little beige coat with the velvet collar and we're off. A cab has been organised to take us home.

In the taxi, Molly starts to grill my dad. 'What was that all about, Ging?' knowing that my dad knows all the nuances of his family's behaviour: big rows and heated outbursts were recurring events over the years.

'Nah, it's nothing,' he sighs. 'OK, I'll tell ya. You won't believe it. She's done it before. She gets all upset because The Old Man carves her a leg. And she really wants the breast.'

I'm old enough to understand how daft this is and start to giggle. My mum, however, is appalled.

'Do you mean to tell me she gets so worked up about a lousy bit of chicken, she has to have a tantrum about it?'

'Yeah. And The Old Man knows pretty much what's gonna happen. But I think he does it just to wind her up.'

So there it is. The country is half starving, still living on rations; even bread is still not yet freely available. Yet my twentysomething aunt looses her cool completely because she gets the wrong part of the chicken on her plate. And, of course, no one else in the family ventures to comment, forever tiptoeing around The Old Man.

To my mum, it highlights the essential difference between her background and my dad's. For years, she remembers the incident and brings it up.

'She cried just because she got a chicken leg,' she'd say, shaking her head and tutting. 'Makes you wonder what she'd do if she had a real problem in life.'

CHAPTER 15
BESIDE THE SEA...

British seaside resorts started to resurface in the early fifties. Until then, posh people and well-off honeymooners went abroad; the rest either went nowhere – or struggled to a nearby coastal resort when the sun came out.

Camping holidays started to be popular and big holiday camps like Butlins, Pontins and Warners began to flourish, places where families could have all their needs catered for under one enormous roof: food, entertainment, someone to look after the kids, all for one price, an all-inclusive week with full board costing around £5 a head in the early fifties, a sum families could save up for throughout the year.

We looked down on Butlins. Far too common. Neither did we save up to go away. We always went to proper hotels in Cliftonville, Kent, places advertised 'with hot-and-cold running water in the bedrooms' (en suite bathrooms were still on the far horizon for such places) and also boasting all-inclusive entertainment: by the mid-fifties Cliftonville hotels like The Cedric or the Oval Court laid on three meals a day plus TV, table tennis, films, dancing and bands, all for six guineas per person (six pounds and six shillings) a week. Bed-and-breakfast guest houses cost much less, two pounds and five shillings a week per person – with a weekend dinner thrown in.

Our annual seaside holidays were often subsidised by the betting fraternity around the Lane, in other words, The Old Man's generosity. My grandparents would book into their favourite hotel for a week or two and my dad's siblings would take it in turns to join them in the hotel for a few days or, for the duration of my grandparents' stay.

In the hotel, The Old Man and a permanently miserable Miriam would hold court, their family around them, while we enjoyed the daytime pleasures of the big sandy beach. At night, after the evening meal, everyone sat in the hotel lounge, a pianist tinkling on the keys in the background while the adults gossiped and chatted over drinks. A bottle of Johnnie Walker Black Label was permanently parked on The Old Man's table, of course.

My dad was never able to come with us for the entire holiday because he'd still be running the betting business back in the Lane. He'd join us for a weekend or the odd day. But really, the whole thing was a perfect example of The Old Man's control over his family: he called the shots and we paid homage.

Cliftonville was not exactly a resort in itself, but a coastal area located in the more respectable part of Margate, Kent, just a couple of miles away from Broadstairs, a much quieter place my parents preferred in later years. But while Broadstairs was as English as its most celebrated resident,

Charles Dickens, Cliftonville hotels in the fifties catered largely to London Jewish families who liked a bit of comfort with their food and entertainment – and relished meeting up with friends and familiar faces from home.

The Old Man's regular chauffeur, Dave, a youngish bloke with crinkly hair and glasses, would park the hired Daimler somewhat incongruously outside our block of flats, collect our cases, load them into the boot and off we'd go, watched through her ground floor window by a hard-faced Maisie, fag in mouth, whose loathing for us and our lifestyle would surely peak at these times.

The drive down to the Kent coast was leisurely, with Dave and my mum chatting about the usual inconsequential things, what the weather would be like, the state of Dave's mum's health, gossip about The Old Man's frequent bust-ups with my grandmother. There were no traffic jams or queues of impatient motorists nose-to-tail then because there were relatively few cars on the road. And a Daimler, of course, the top people's car at the time, gave you a very luxurious ride with its plush quilted red leather seats to sink back into and loads of enticing-looking dials on the dashboard.

'I was outside in the car and I could hear her out the window, screaming at 'im,' Dave would tell my mum.

'I dunno why she's so jealous of 'im. It's not as if he's one for goin' after the wimmin. He'd rather be in the pub. Know what? I reckon 'e's in the pub all the time to get away from 'er!'

Miriam's jealous passion for The Old Man was consistent, unrelenting, the talk of the Lane. It never ever stopped. It ruined her relationship with her offspring, even when they were small, because her sole focus was Jack, what Jack was doing, what he might be doing, how much he might be drinking, what time he came back from the pub or, worse, whether he was chatting up Another Woman. All her emotional output went into her obsession with Jack. Tragically, the result of this was that scant maternal affection was bestowed on the children; they'd been brought up mostly by aunts, because Miriam had worked alongside Jack in their coal shop while her children grew up. When the business focus switched, for some reason, from coal to betting just before the war, the jealousy darkened: betting, with all its attendant ducking and diving on the street and contact in pubs meant that unlike in the shop, she couldn't keep an eye on hubby all the time, hence their somewhat crazy move to Petticoat Lane during the Blitz years.

Now, both in their sixties, the hard war years behind them, their children grown up and settled, it could have been a good time to let up, relax, enjoy the fruits of Jack's dodgy labours. But even on those seaside trips, Miriam would be stern, her smooth pink face never breaking into a smile, her white hair piled up in a bun, her black beaver lamb coat on her lap (somewhat incongruous in the summer months but this was England, after all), her big black leather handbag parked on the table. Impassive at best, usually simmering with resentment by her hubby's side, she would glare at any woman who might venture to talk to her man or engage him in conversation.

Since Jack's main preoccupation was Black Label, it was usually the hotel waitress or barmaid who got it in the neck. Even if they did nothing at all but serve.

'Just put it down and piss off!' she'd tell the bemused girl trying to lay out the contents of a tray laden with cups and saucers for the couple's after-dinner lemon tea, no milk.

The Old Man, of course, would pretend to ignore all this. That was the public face of their relationship. Indoors, it was heavy duty, really nasty screaming matches, according to legend. But outwardly, socially, they were A Happy Couple, Darby and Joan. And he, at least, though as undemonstrative as his missus in terms of open signs of affection for his family, had reached the stage in life where he'd slowed down and appreciated what he had. As I've said, I wasn't the kind of kid who'd deliberately engage with him, perch on his lap or ask to play with his fob watch. But he eventually began to relish this sort of engagement and encouraged it when other grandchildren came along in his later years.

Most kids' memories of seaside holidays are idyllic: mine are similar. The tensions and shortcomings of adult relationships couldn't diminish the sheer joy of the whole thing, simply because we were in such a different environment, far away from the grit and grime of Dalston. When it was fine, you went to the beach clutching your bucket and spade, dug around in the sand for hours, made usually lopsided sandcastles, ran in and out of the water, splashed around and hunted, for ages, when the tide was out, for interesting looking shells.

All this was sheer heaven for an inner-city child, the only point in my childhood when I had anything like a link with nature and the elements. And my brief career as a performer moved up a notch on these holidays: even the unfortunate Rat episode didn't diminish my enthusiasm for stepping up to the stage. In the evenings, I'd often wind up reciting or singing in the hotel, at the microphone in my white organdie dress with its big frill and red velvet trim, mostly tolerated ('another spoilt kid') by the other holidaymaking families and their kids, none of whom I chummed up with. A self-contained and spoilt little girl, certainly, but with books, reading and words for sustenance, by now I had my own little world to sustain my imagination and feed my thirst for some sort of self expression.

Watching me perform on those holidays, Mum would glow with happiness and pride at my facility for words. So they were, as summer holidays should be, good times for us. Perhaps the sun didn't actually shine every day. But it didn't matter, though my memory now is only of sunny days and childish pleasures. For I was at my happiest then, secure in my own little bubble: an only child who was used to getting all the attention. As they say, what was not to like?

CHAPTER 16
THE GOOD FRIDAY
AGREEMENT

I am tucked up under the blankets in my little bedroom. It is late, but I am not yet ready to sleep because my dad has just come in from work for a goodnight kiss. But I, of course, about five years old, want more from him, this man who has travelled so far across the world. 'Tell me about India, Daddy,' I ask and he obliges, yet again, with the stories I love hearing: the weeks spent in rough, perilous conditions on the huge troopship, escorted by destroyers all the way across the Indian Ocean to Bombay; the huge shock of the intense, searing heat as the troopship arrived through The Gateway to India – 'just like going to the Turkish baths but worse'; getting used to being called 'pukka sahib' (Hindi slang for true gentleman) by the Indian helpers; watching the Indian mess boys knead the dough for the troops' food with their bare feet; how the searing heat would actually melt the coating on the carbons they'd use for copying their work.

These snippets of information from this exotic, far-off world, never failed to set my imagination on fire. 'More,

Daddy, more,' I plead. For in my childish world, these extraordinary tales of distant, hot, mysterious places make my dad unique, special, a giant amongst men. No one else had done the things he'd done, had they?

Like many kids, I don't see that much of my father. He works six days a week, often arriving home by the time I'm asleep, only joining us for the odd day or two on seaside holidays. Even on Sundays, he is only home for part of the day and then he's usually asleep. My mum, of course, is my permanent anchor, warm and loving, always there. But because I see him in brief snatches, understandably I hang out for precious quality time alone with my dad. Can't he take me out one day, just the two of us, somewhere nice? By now, I've developed a bit of a habit of nagging him about this, whenever I spot a chance.

'OK,' he says, after I've asked him to take me out somewhere for the umpteenth time. 'It's Good Friday coming up and there's no racing, so I'll take you out, I promise. How about we go on the bus down to the Tower of London?'

I'm thrilled to bits, can't believe my luck. I know that we live just two bus rides away from the historic heart of London, but the prospect of a trip to see the Tower with its Beefeaters and ghostly past – every kid then knew the Stanley Holloway song 'With her 'ead tucked underneath her arm', which told the story of how the ghost of the beheaded Anne Boleyn haunts the Tower – is exciting. Especially if I'm going there with my dad.

Soon he closes my door and I snuggle under the blankets and drift off to sleep, one happy little girl, buoyed by the promise of this longed-for outing.

The next morning, I'm already on the case.

'Dad's taking me to the Tower!' I tell my mum, who's in the kitchen, washing up.

'We're going on Good Friday!'

At that moment, my dad emerges from their bedroom. He's dressed for work, smart, perfectly pressed suit trousers, neatly ironed shirt, patterned silk tie. His clothes are immaculate – he's very careful about his appearance, like my mum – but he looks pale, somewhat bleary. He's in Bad Hangover territory, the place he inhabits virtually every day. But, of course, at five years old, I don't have a clue about this.

'Dad! When's it Good Friday?' I prattle innocently. 'When we gonna go to the Tower?'

My dad looks at me blankly.

'What Tower? Whatya talkin' about? And where's my cufflinks, Mol?' he asks my mum.

'Can't find 'em anywhere.'

'Tower of London,' I repeat, still not getting it. 'We're gonna go to the Tower on Good Friday, you said, Dad.'

But my dad doesn't respond. I'm bewildered at this but I'm silent, pensive. Something is very, very wrong and I can't work out what it is. My mum, meanwhile, has gone into the bedroom to rummage around and, in a flash, she's back with the missing cufflinks which she dutifully hands to her husband.

'Leave your dad alone, Jac,' she says, seeing my puzzled little face.

By now, I'm sucking my thumb, a baby habit that I don't relinquish until a few years later. It's a sign I'm confused or troubled.

'Dad's gotta go to work now. We'll talk about Good Friday later on,' she tells me as the front door closes behind my dad.

But we never do. And I never have that outing to the Tower with my dad: it was never going to happen in the first place. My father was sozzled, pissed, well and truly inebriated that night; he'd made his promise to me after a heavy night in the pub. And in the morning, of course, he didn't remember a word of it, let alone that he'd made a promise. Nor did he wish to be reminded. When drunk, who knows, maybe he saw himself as the man he hoped to be: a kindly, loving dad who took his little girl out on a rare day off work? But in the cold light of day, when more or less sober, he didn't have the time or inclination for that sort of thing: my mum was there for all that. His role was to get out there and bring in the readies to pay for everything. That was the deal.

I don't know precisely when it actually dawned on me that my dad's promise had been broken because he was drunk and didn't remember a thing about it the next day. But the Good Friday Incident proved to be the real turning point in my relationship with my father, the point when he went from being a hero of sorts to someone who would let you down, make a promise and break it. It's a rotten thing to do to a child. And I was sensitive enough for it to affect me permanently.

Gradually, over time, I became increasingly conscious of my dad's drinking habit and how it changed him, turned him into a person I didn't like – and eventually didn't want to know. The big wedding incident had been a very public demonstration of how shaming he could be socially – but by the time that happened, I'd already started to work it all out. Sober, he was quite grumpy and morose (it was really a permanent hangover). But after several double scotches, he was a horrible, noisy, loudmouthed stranger. The sort of person you didn't want to be around, let alone live with. And I never went anywhere or did anything with my dad, just the two of us, until I'd reached adulthood and actually left home. Even then, it proved to be a rare event: by that time I couldn't stand to be in his company for more than an hour or so.

Growing up like this, in a very small, cramped flat, meant that it was very difficult to escape from both the day-to-day reality of living with someone whose life was dominated by alcohol – apart from the constantly overheard conversations and exchanges between my parents in their bedroom, I'd frequently hear my dad retching his guts out in the bathroom – and from my own jumble of intense feelings about it all. I didn't understand it; what child does? And I couldn't blank it out, ignore it at all or hide in another part of our home because it was so tiny, so claustrophobic. Talk about nowhere to run. It was there, all the time, year in, year out, two men living in our home – one grumpy, hungover and struggling to function, the other occasionally effusive, loud, boisterous, but increasingly as time passed, verbally abusive, explosive and very, very angry at the world. Even now I have younger relatives who fondly remember my dad's social face: funny, generous, lively and outgoing. 'Street angel, house devil,' is my response to this. You had to live with it to know it.

In today's terms my dad wasn't just a heavy drinker – he was an alcoholic. Drink was a permanent crutch to get him through. But then, of course, such terms were never bandied about. Some men just drank more than others. And my dad was far from alone in his struggle to use booze to adjust to post-war life and responsibilities he couldn't quite accept. There were plenty of other people in pubs matching him drink for drink. My dad's siblings knew all about his excess drinking of course. But he was more or less accepted, with a shrug, as the family black sheep. Every family had one, didn't they? And they'd grown up alongside The Old Man's drinking, though none of them, apart from my dad, developed the pub habit in any way.

As for my mum, she'd always known the youthful Ginger as a bit of a drinker, though he'd been more of a happy drunk when they were young. And he probably had less cash to fling around on whisky in their early courting days. Now, she was stuck with it, lived with it. Her compensation was our bizarre financial security – and me. So rather than become bitter or aggrieved – like my grandmother, who became overwhelmed with bitterness and permanent resentment about Jack's Drinking – she immersed herself in the joy of what she loved, a sane approach given the circumstances. It made life easier. Had she confronted him or challenged his behaviour things would have been a lot worse all round.

Throughout the fifties, our little home started to change. Our flat began to show the material evidence of what was happening outside – the country's slowly emerging consumerism. My mum wasn't especially house-proud, aspiring to a comfortable and carefully thought out home. She just went out and bought whatever big item we needed after my dad had handed over the money. First came the seventeen-inch TV set from Bardens on Kingsland High Street, bought on hire purchase. Each week she would march down to Bardens and pay off the l6/6d (sixteen shillings and sixpence) weekly payment, spread over two years. My dad could have easily handed over cash for the set, around £70, then. But he liked the idea of the new HP; it appealed to his sense of 'have it now, pay up later'. And so my mum was able to replace the somewhat shabby utility post-war furnishings in our flat with brand new furniture: a three-piece moquette lounge suite, at £40 (just seven shillings and nine pence a week), and, for their bedroom, a £60 walnut mahogany bedroom suite at eleven shillings a week from Davants down the road, as well as a new dark-green fitted carpet to cover the grim and ancient lino in the hall and living room. For some reason, probably because they didn't have a clue about hiring a decent local fitter to lay a brand new carpet – they certainly couldn't do it themselves – the carpet was poorly fitted. And it remained as it was. Getting value for money or a good job done didn't figure with either of my parents. You paid. And if you got a bad job, you shrugged and lived with it. It wasn't that important.

We acquired a fridge from the local North Thames Gas Board showroom, also on the 'never-never' (long-term credit), another eight bob (eight shillings) a week. The fridge was a tiny box by today's standards but it worked. Processed cheese squares wrapped in silver paper, nestling in their little round box are an early memory of what we kept inside our first fridge. And, of course, the new frozen foods – things like peas and fish fingers were popped into the tiny freezer section at the top.

The TV, however, was a technical disaster. Getting it to work needed considerable patience. The picture was often fuzzy and, no matter what you did with the indoor aerial, there were frustrating nights trying to get it to work properly if you wanted to watch programmes like *What's My Line?* (I was somewhat fascinated by a rather rude man called Gilbert Harding, a permanent fixture on the show, perhaps because his big glasses reminded me of The Old Man) or even the puppet *Muffin the Mule* (which I thought was silly; I wasn't a kid for puppets or even dolls).

Often, we'd wind up peering at the screen, trying to watch a programme while horizontal lines ran right across the set or there was some other form of major interference. Yet no matter how dodgy the picture, after the coronation in '53, Britain's telly habit really took off. Even if you wound up stuck with nothing but the Test Card, the permanent fixture on the screen between programmes. Viewing hours were very limited in those early days, until commercial telly got going after the mid-fifties.

Around this time we also acquired what became my dad's most cherished possession: a proper cocktail cabinet, which took pride of place in the corner of the living room. This too was bought on the never-never, courtesy of our high street; it was an ugly, shiny edifice with a pull-down handle that revealed the full works, the bottles of sherry, advocaat, gin, whisky, brandy and Babycham and the accompanying little cocktail glasses with plastic cocktail sticks, all lit up by an internal light. It was all incredibly sophisticated. But since we rarely entertained, it never got used unless my parents had a drink before stepping out for a big night.

Our cleaner, Annie, arrived each week to do very little except moan about everything and everyone, wielding a duster for a brief half hour, thus 'earning' her two-and-sixpence. My mum was always complaining about her, after she'd left. In those days, there was no Dyson or Henry to whizz round the floor, but a rather pathetic carpet sweeper, which didn't really do the job. Nor was Annie's 'dusting' up to much. If it did get vigorous and my mum and I had gone out briefly, it usually meant returning to damage.

'I can't believe it, she's broken something AGAIN,' Molly would wail, holding up the remains of a ceramic ashtray, new ornament or cup.

'I'd swear she does it on purpose.'

Annie had a big family, about six kids, and a layabout husband who always seemed to be home sick or out of work. My mum felt sorry for her and was just too kind to go the whole hog and sack her. Nor did she dare dock Annie's wages for the breakages or bother to tell my dad about her shortcomings. And so she 'cleaned' for us every Friday morning for several years, only resigning when the authorities finally rehoused the family in far-off Dagenham, much to my mum's relief. And despite my dad's encouragement, Annie was not replaced. My mum said she could manage the dusting and a proper Hoover vacuum cleaner was eventually acquired, also paid off in a two-year repayment deal.

We needed to keep some of our home intact, after all.

CHAPTER 17
THE ELVIS YEARS

I am conjuring up magical powers on stage – in Stoke Newington. I don't know it but this is my swansong as a child performer, playing the sorcerer's apprentice in my last ever primary school concert at the Town Hall.

The concert, set to a scratchy recording of classical music, is based on a segment of *Fantasia*, the animated hit Disney movie of the 1940s, with Mickey Mouse playing a youthful apprentice magician who creates magic he can't control. And I'm very conscious of my power, immensely pleased with myself, as I stride onto the stage in my apprentice costume, waving my axe, summoning up mysterious elements I don't understand and creating havoc – until my cloaked master with the pointy wizard hat returns to set things right.

'Don't mess around with things you don't understand' is the useful metaphor for the piece. Yet this, somehow, is lost on me. It is the storytelling itself, the dramatic effect of live performance, spouting words set to powerful music that has me in thrall. But when the overenthusiastic clapping of the admiring audience of mums and dads fades away, so does my performing career. For I am now about to step up to grammar school. I've passed the Eleven Plus exam with flying colours. A glorious future awaits me…

'Skinners', glorious Skinners' were the opening words of my new school song. Well… it was glorious for some. It certainly had illustrious origins: The Skinners' Company's School for Girls was founded by the Worshipful Company of Skinners, one of the oldest of London's medieval Trade Guilds, or Livery Companies.

Housed in a Victorian building on Stamford Hill, this was a grammar school that placed sporting excellence above academic achievement, which naturally had me right out of the picture from day one. And my brief stint there – just over three years – proved to be a total flop, a bit of a disaster. From hero to zero. Within a year of arrival in September 1956 – the same year that Elvis started to make shockwaves around the world – I'd morphed from the swot child, the eager performer who'd never been kissed, didn't yet use lipstick or wear a bra, into a sulky, sarky Elvis-mad teenager who'd lost all interest in performing – or study.

At primary, I'd remained, somewhat obsessively, at the top of my class every year. My final school report said: 'Shows outstanding ability in any form of written expression.' Hopes for my future soared. Call it puberty, call it lack of a competitive spirit – I'd had little competition at primary from my premier league niche – but once placed with a group of equally bright girls of my own age, I simply stopped bothering. And I became a mess: wild, uncombed hair, school skirt pocket stuffed with rubbish, relentlessly taking the mickey out of the teachers, sarcastic, pretty insolent much of the time. I didn't have much respect for authority – or the chance to learn. And it really showed.

Certainly, the Skinners' teachers were a very different bunch to the ones I'd known at Princess May. These had been mostly kind, enthusiastic if you showed aptitude and more or less seemed to quite enjoy their work, even if they did have to teach classes of nearly fifty kids in a tough East London environment.

Skinners' teachers were more formal, maiden aunt spinster types with cropped hair. They wore stiff tweedy suits with box-pleated skirts. A few of the younger ones were pleasant and communicative. Yet the majority were older, mannish looking or academic, remote characters, inhabitants of a somewhat cloistered, middle-class world very far away from the rough and tumble of the East End.

Now, of course, I understand more about the backdrop to their lives: mostly well-bred, privately educated women from a very different era. Free secondary education for girls only became available to all after World War II and before that, teaching itself had been one of the very few professions open to women. But not only were female teachers very badly paid, they were often asked to resign if they married. So it really was the unmarried woman's career choice.

Yet real social change, especially for women, was now on the horizon. The Pill was just a few years away. The office jobs market was poised to boom. And while our teachers were trained to teach girls who were bright and had real potential, in the case of my year onwards there was a bit of a problem: our interests were being fired, as never before, by all manner of huge consumer-led distractions, the big ones being the start of rock'n'roll (Bill Hailey, he of the ridiculous kiss curl, had already launched the era with 'Rock Around the Clock' in 1954), which coincided with the arrival of the record player and the telly and, of course, the dawn of the worldwide phenomenon that was Elvis. How could these women, from a world of genteel, polite spinsterdom, possibly hope to hold our attention, compete against all that?

'STAND, CREATURE!'

This was the usual form of address from the Latin teacher, Miss McLelland. Political correctness was a long, long way ahead of us. Teachers like McLelland, a dark-haired woman in her late forties, made no attempt whatsoever to conceal their disdain for their charges.

'COME TO THE FLOOR, CREATURE!'

I've been caught red-handed. Stupidly, I thought I was safe right at the back of the classroom. But her beady, ever-vigilant eye has spotted me, trying to pass a Harold Robbins book to a giggling Annie Black under the desk. But while my class teacher, Miss Edgar, an English instructor wasn't a stern disciplinarian, especially with those who demonstrated signs of an affinity with language, Miss McLelland gave no quarter to anyone. Older than many of the other teachers, she had a fan club of none – primarily because everyone hated Latin and couldn't wait for the lessons to end.

'Latin is a language as dead as dead can be/ It killed the Ancient Romans/ And now it's killing me' one bored wag had scratched onto one of our old wooden desks. And it was true. I didn't mind French. But Latin was beyond the pale.

'CAN YOU SHOW US WHAT YOU'RE READING, CREATURE?'

I shrug. 'Dunno Miss McLelland. Found it on the bus.'

'HAND IT OVER, CREATURE!'

Grudgingly, I hand over the offending paperback, which she flicks through, winces then holds aloft at the class.

'NEVER/LOVE/A/STRANGER,' she says, pronouncing each word with pure venom.

A few brave souls snigger. I'm done for, yet again. Another detention, my second that week. I am way, way up high on her list of Most Detested Creatures.

'LEAVE THE ROOM, CREATURE AND WAIT OUTSIDE!'

The trouble was, I didn't give a monkey's. There was no remorse whatsoever. At least, in primary school, when I'd got into hot water for pulling the huge plaits of my rival for scholarly supremacy, Valerie Neal, another swot who had the misfortune to be fat, a total affront to my senses, I'd felt mortified after the event. I floundered to find one but I had no excuse, I'd just given into a really bad impulse. Yet at Skinners' I experienced no guilt at all for constantly being called out, being disruptive – the teacher's oft repeated description of my attitude. And, of course, I was always a sitting target for getting caught. Other equally cheeky girls managed to stay on the right side of the teachers because they cleverly operated the two-faced technique: devils in the playground when authority wasn't around, seemingly angelic in class when it was (a useful survival tactic for office life too, though one I never learned at work, either). I never bothered with subterfuge.

As far as I was concerned our teachers were a joke, ancient, from the Dark Ages, something else to laugh about, sneer at.

Learning, alas, was no longer my pleasure, though I was still keen on books and read avidly. And big-selling US fiction authors like Harold Robbins who wrote of risqué topics like prostitution were bound to be of interest: at that stage, of course, any mention of anything remotely sexual was likely to be pored over – it was the only kind of sex education available. And Robbins' books didn't hold back…one of the few commercially successful authors of the era who made millions by writing about relationships in vivid prose.

And yet my folks had been so chuffed when I'd passed the Eleven Plus. Various options were discussed. Even stage school was mooted. The Old Man had been consulted. He'd suggested I try for the City of London School for Girls, a prestigious school, founded in the late 1800s. It would have meant passing a stiff exam for a scholarship, but I didn't pass the initial interview. So they plumped for sending me to another well-regarded school, Skinners', a twenty-minute bus ride up through Stoke Newington to Stamford Hill.

'The Hill' was considerably posher than our part of the world. It boasted a park, some smart shops and many big Victorian houses. Then, as now, there were many Jewish families living there. And my parents, somewhat naively, believed that because Skinners' had a high proportion of Jewish pupils – over half the total population of my year – this was bound to be 'better' for my education.

How wrong can you be? The exposure to more Jewish pupils meant rubbing shoulders with girls who were from wealthier backgrounds, had travelled, were more sophisticated and were, in some cases, quite precocious. Despite our comparative affluence at home, until then, my primary-school buddies had been girls from working-class families, quite different to some of the posher Skinners' girls who were already well into rock'n'roll and boy chasing.

My two main primary school chums, Sandra Holland and Kathy Shilling, lived in shabby rented houses off the Kingsland Road, their parents' lives were modest, respectable – but they were quite unworldly. And our joint exploits – making a bonfire night Guy and standing on the corner of Kingsland Road asking passers-by for pennies (a challenge I relished, truth to tell, despite my parents' horror that I was out on the street 'begging') – were distinctly childish.

Some of these new Skinners' classmates seemed daring to me, already wearing nylons and lipstick out of school; one or two even had boyfriends a few years older than them. These girls' influence made a big impression on me. And this, combined with the fact that we were among the first group of teenagers to emerge as post-war teenagers with consumerist leanings, developing our own tastes and clothes, rather than remaining just younger, drab versions of our parents until adulthood, meant I was never going to take education seriously.

At home, my parents' ambitions for me beyond getting into Skinners' and forking out for the nice red-and-grey uniform (which could only be purchased from Kinch & Lack, a shop specialising in school uniforms near Victoria Station) were distinctly hazy.

'Is fifty quid enough? queried Ginger, peeling off the notes as if they were playing cards to purchase the new uniform. They'd both left school at fourteen, my mum an avowed duffer who had relied on her elder siblings to help crib her homework. For them, passing the exam was a huge achievement in itself. Yet the whole point of the Eleven Plus was for bright working-class kids to be streamed, a big step on a path that could, if they worked really hard, lead to university and a real chance in life for the ordinary, less privileged child.

But in my case, as the actress Carrie Fisher once said: great anecdote, bad reality. With my dad permanently sloshed most nights and my mum vainly trying to keep a fragile peace between us – open warfare between me and Ginger really got going when I hit my teens – they just weren't likely to put all their efforts into helping me understand that this was A Big Opportunity. Their own 'live for now' horizons were too limited. And I was a temperamental child, hard to handle, prone to outbursts. Moreover, I was reasonably pretty, quite slim, with no major defects. They blithely assumed I'd probably be married by the time I passed my teens.

So there you have some idea why the great post-war social experiment that was the Eleven Plus didn't work out for the education of one kid from Hackney.

Though you must never discount the distraction of the powerful cultural influences creeping up on us all, especially Elvis, whose voice, sexual charisma and astonishing good looks had us nudging hysteria at the Regent cinema on the Hill when *Love Me Tender*, Elvis' first movie, lit up the screen. We'd scream to order every time he curled his lip or did his bump 'n' grind routine. Though on reflection, the majority of us, still barely adults, didn't really have a clue exactly why he turned us on so much.

CHAPTER 18

ONE NIGHT OF SHAME

By the end of that first year I'd already teamed up with a few of the more worldly Skinners' girls; many of them travelled on my bus route home. There were the sisters, Sylvie and Barbara, just eighteen months apart, one cheerful and sunny, the other sullen and brooding. Their parents were rumoured to have separated, something so rare and shocking then that the sisters never talked about it openly.

Sylvie was friendly, gregarious and tried really hard in class, though she never got great marks, no matter how assiduously she worked. Barbara, the older sister, was morose, scruffy, in a permanent sulk, though with a cutting wit and, underneath the unappealing exterior, extremely bright: she'd get good marks without much study. Linda, Heather and Rosalind made up their gang, a tight little trio already plotting their way to courtship and marriage to local boys met at the nearby Stamford Hill Club, a social meeting place for young Jewish kids. Heather, with huge eyes and blonde hair, already had an older steady beau, Mike. I latched on to these girls partly because they were more knowing and worldly, partly for good company on the bus. But I wasn't consistently part of their group, perhaps because I sensed I didn't have a real affinity with them. Their focus, even at that early stage, was snaring a Jewish husband, which to me seemed a bit remote – and short-sighted. And before long, I'd bonded with another Hackney girl in my year who eventually became my best friend, Larraine, widely known as Lolly, thanks to a hit Chordettes song of '58 called 'Lollipop', which went 'Lollipop, Lollipop, ooh Lolli, Lolli, Lolli', an embarrassment for her when other kids burst into song and chanted it. But while the song came and went in the charts, the nickname stuck.

We were quite different too but the bonds grew from our shared interests, mainly books, clothes and Elvis records, with a growing interest in the opposite sex, though like me, Lolly hadn't yet reached the actual boyfriend stage.

She was the eldest of three kids, growing up on a council estate. Her dad Monty was a London cabbie, something that proved to be a bit of a bonus later on when we started hanging around clubs and coffee houses in the West End. In appearance, we were opposite: she dark-haired, tiny and exotic looking, me, taller, fair-skinned and freckled. There were other differences. Lolly firmly believed my mum to be 'posh' because she spoke nicely and dressed like a movie star, while Larraine's mum Fay, equally attractive, was very earthy, quite loud with a distinct East End Jewish twang.

This belief that somehow I had a more upmarket status was confirmed for Lolly the afternoon she first came round to our flat and my mum offered her a drink, instant coffee, spooned out from a tin of Nescafé.

My new friend had never seen this kind of coffee before.

'Ooh, thanks Mrs Hyams,' she said, taking the cup and very much impressed by the novelty of something different.

'We only have Camp coffee at home, this is lovely.' Molly looked quizzical: she'd heard of Camp, knew it was much cheaper – but in our world of cash bribes and never-never payments, who would think of actually buying it?

(Camp Coffee was a thick brown liquid made out of water, sugar, chicory essence and a little bit of coffee essence, a popular inexpensive coffee substitute in the austerity years, with its distinctive bottle showing a Scottish and a Sikh soldier sitting by a tent. It's still around now: people use it in baking to give a coffee flavour.)

The next day, Lolly told me she thought I had a lot more going for me than she did. 'Your mum's so posh. She's really ladylike. And you don't live on a council estate, like us,' she reminded me.

'Yeah, but it's a dump,' was my retort.

'And my mum's not really posh. She's just got lots of nice clothes.'

We differed in one other respect: Lolly and her siblings adored both their parents, yet I had an open aversion to my dad whose ridiculous possessiveness had started to increase as I got older, though I kept fairly quiet about my embarrassment about his drinking. Lolly couldn't do exactly what she liked. But with two other children in their flat, she had slightly more freedom than me.

I loved the very different environment in their noisily

cheerful home. With a plump, boisterous ten-year-old brother, Keith, and a quieter younger sister, Adrienne, with whom she shared a bedroom, their three-bedroom council flat near Mare Street was bigger and livelier, with family members popping in and out all the time. It was nothing like my world, without visitors or space, sticking fast to my books and my damp little room facing the noisy timberyard when my dad was around, permanently avoiding him and only feeling happy to move around the flat when he wasn't there.

So I spent quite a lot of after-school time at Lolly's, ostensibly doing 'homework' (which initially involved minimal effort and plunged to near zero within a year or so) but mainly listening to Elvis on her much-prized green leatherette Dansette record player, purchased by her dad in Mare Street, or swapping passages or poems from books we'd liked, laboriously copying them down by hand, then cutting out each passage and sticking it into a scrapbook. We repeated the process with our treasured Elvis pictures. Magazine photos were starting to appear of him in various guises, on stage in a velvet shirt, reaching out to his fans, bare-chested, looking moodily into the distance.

Some of these photos went onto our bedroom walls, despite parental objection, but most went into the precious scrapbooks. And it was only Elvis. We didn't have much choice – Frankie Laine, anyone? – but we weren't fickle. No one else but Elvis really got a look in.

The Hill had a few attractions for soppy teenage girls in search of laughs and adventure. It had an amusement arcade – known as 'the schtip' – where older boys hung out and the E & A bar, a salt beef bar where we could buy huge pickled cucumbers to munch on as we walked around after school, giggling with our gaggle of cronies before getting on the bus, climbing upstairs and creating havoc.

Skinners' rules were strict: no eating outside the school premises or on the street, no venturing into the local shops. A few obedient swots obeyed but most of us ignored this. Though it was easy to spot Skinners' girls because of the uniform, envied throughout the area: a very slick red-and-black striped blazer, red stripey cotton blouse tucked into a grey wool skirt, grey or black socks, Mary Jane one-strap shoes or lace-ups. In winter we wore a grey V-neck jumper with a red border over the blouse. There was also a nasty grey beret, usually shoved in my pocket, and a grey belted mac – which didn't get worn much. At other secondary schools, like Laura Place in nearby Clapton, the uniforms were grim: everything brown. How many teenage girls want to wear brown knickers?

But while I already had an awareness of clothes and what they could do for you, mainly thanks to my mum, when it came to boys, I was nowhere – no brothers, male cousins, other than Anthony who didn't count, or even girlfriends with brothers. And, since I'd gone to an all-girls primary, boys remained a huge mystery. Yet some of the girls in my class had already started to experience those first ever kisses and sexual fumbles – and talked about it openly.

Naturally, this troubled me greatly. Was there something wrong with me? And how did you behave around boys? I had no idea. Lolly and I would discuss the boys we liked the look of endlessly. But getting up close and personal with them was another thing. OK, you'd 'know' boys locally, their names, where they lived, who their friends were, where they hung around – the same places as us, mainly in and around the local Jewish club near the Hill or around the E & A bar, but you didn't exactly go beyond smiles, the occasional nod hello or 'look'.

Only if a boy came up to you at a local club dance – there were no discos then – and asked you to dance could you start to communicate in any way. The breakthrough point, of course, was if they asked to see you home. But the rule was you waited for them to ask. Girls didn't even dance together; it was a time of wait and he will come. Eventually. There were things like table tennis at the Jewish club that had ice-breaking potential. But, of course, I eschewed anything remotely sporty. So I wasn't going to get anywhere there.

In that first year at Skinners', I had another big hang-up: I didn't yet need to wear a bra. Oh, the shame. Not having tits was a serious black mark against me, reducing the possibilities of attracting a boy. Lolly already wore a bra. But I still had nothing to speak of up top. So with a bit of encouragement from Lolly, I decided to cheat. Without my mum knowing, I went into Dudleys, the big department store on the corner of Kingsland Road, and artfully purchased a pair of 'falsies' with my pocket money, two useful bits of foam padding which, when deployed under a jumper, would give the illusion of a comely shape.

It might have been a good idea to have actually worn them. Because there was one unforgettable winter's night at the Stamford Hill club which was to go down in history as My Night of Unbelievable Shame.

Lolly and I more or less copied each other when it came to fashion. If she had a new fully-fashioned button-through cardigan from Marks & Spencer, I'd get one too, though from a different shop because I thought M&S was too common, too many people wore it. And you couldn't try things on. Lolly, more practical, liked the M&S convenience factor, with its returns policy on production of the receipt (they were light years ahead of all other high street retailers on this). And, in our desire to look more sophisticated, we'd both recently acquired inexpensive but quite wide heavy wicker basket bags, open at the top without any sort of fastening, so you could hook the basket onto your arm, aiming to look chic. And it was very easy to just put your hand in to fish for a purse, a mirror or, rarely in my case, a comb.

On the night in question, I've popped my falsies into my basket a few days before. But as I stand there in the club, chatting to Lolly, basket on arm, cautiously eyeing the boys, I'm taken by surprise. Unexpectedly, an older boy we know by name, Roy Gordon, appears alongside us, grinning. Then he suddenly dips his hand into my basket – and, horror of horrors, out come my falsies, bundled up with an elastic band. Pay dirt! (He'd probably expected, at best, a lipstick to muck around with.)

'Whoooah, whatcha, got in there!' yells Roy in triumph, pulling off the elastic band and waving the falsies aloft for everyone in the room to see.

'Give 'em back!' I screech, panicking like mad. But it's far too late. A delighted Roy is now parading himself around the clubroom, stuffing the falsies under his jumper, prowling round the room in a parody of a girls' walk.

'Didn't think you needed THESE!

'Look everyone, Jacky Hyams wants to show you her tits!'

Shame isn't in it. I am utterly, totally mortified. Any bit of fake confidence I might pretend to have has been totally demolished. For thirty seconds, I just stand there, rooted to the spot, going redder and redder, awash with embarrassment. Lolly can't help; she doesn't know what to do or say either. And by now, of course, everyone around has got the joke and is laughing fit to bust, if you'll pardon the pun. My humiliation is complete.

Back home, I chuck the foolish falsies down the smelly chute. And after that, whenever we see Roy at the club, he smirks knowingly, makes a snide comment – 'gotcha falsies tonight, Jack?' – and all I can do is manage a 'piss off' to him before moving as far away as possible. Can't he ever let me forget it?

Yet within a few months everything has changed: I've miraculously sprouted tiny boobs. Molly helps me choose a Kayser Bondor bra in Jax, on the Kingsland Road, plus a very grown-up suspender belt to keep up my first-ever pair of stockings. (Kayser Bondor is one of the leading, much advertised underwear brands of the fifties.) OK, I still haven't been kissed. But at long last, to my mind, I am really growing up…

CHAPTER 19
THE IDEAL HOME

A summer Saturday and Molly and I are on a train, going to Leicester for a reunion of sorts, an old friend, a woman called Edie with whom she'd worked in Oxford Street during the war.

This is intriguing, a strange place with people we'd never seen. Or heard of, come to that. By now, early teens, I am old enough to resist attempts by my parents to get me to keep up the regular Sunday visits down the Lane to my grandparents. This causes rows, of course. I suspect my mother is sympathetic to my early rebellion but she continues to back my dad.

'You've got to see them, it's all about RESPECT!' Ginger yells.

'I don't care. I don't want to go there, I'm sick of going there. There's a funny atmosphere, anyway.'

'Whaddya mean by that? What "atmosphere"? What's she talkin' about Mol?' says my dad, handing it over to my mum in the hope she can sort it.

'I don't know, Ging. Look Jac, they're your grandparents.

You have to go.'

'NO I DON'T,' I scream, running into my bedroom, slamming the door hard behind me. (How that door remained on its hinges is a mystery; perhaps workmanship, as is often claimed, really was better in the thirties.)

Sometimes I win this battle, sometimes I don't. But my rejection of anything to do with my dad is like a running sore through our lives. I can't articulate it, it's just there, a feeling, a sense that I need to disassociate myself with anything to do with the Lane, his life – and, of course, the boozing.

To me, the whole package stinks. And I'm not making it up about 'the atmosphere'. There are times when we visit the flat in Stoney Lane that you can sense a brooding tension, waiting to explode – which means my grandparents are about to have yet another major ding-dong, and they're already locked into one of their 'not speaking to each other' modes. Who wanted to be around that?

But today's little adventure holds promise, a journey into the unknown. The train seems to take ages. But when we alight, Edie is waiting for us at the barrier, ecstatic to see us. She's quite plump, untidy, carelessly dressed in a shapeless printed frock and tatty cardi; she's the same age as my mum, but she looks much older, more careworn. But she's got a little car, a Morris Minor, and we pile in for the short journey to her terraced house with Edie at the wheel, telling us about her job serving in a local newsagents – 'the money's bad but the owner's wife is good to me' – her misfortune at being recently widowed – 'Poor old Wally, never was the same after he came back from Burma' – and her two kids, Paul and Dawn, older than me and already working.

'Wait till you meet them,' she tells me.

'You'll get on like a house on fire.'

Dawn, sixteen, is at the front door to greet us. As cheerful and friendly as her mum, she's got a round, pleasant face, dark blonde hair in a pony tail and she's wearing a neat pleated skirt with a button-down cardigan. 'Ooh, I like your skirt,' she tells me, admiring my more fashionable London gear: brightly coloured dirndl skirt with large appliqué pattern, white blouse with three-quarter-length sleeves and beige suede flatties.

I'm instantly interested in this older girl, already out in the world, as we're ushered into a small but very neat, spick-and-span living room. Unlike our flat with its bare walls, they have lots of framed prints hanging up, mostly landscapes. And there are loads of cushions and pretty ornaments. It's cosy, welcoming. Then mother and daughter disappear into the kitchen, clattering around, readying our high tea.

And then it happens. A young man walks in.

'I'm so pleased to meet you at last, Mum never stops talking about you, Molly,' he says, shaking Molly's hand and then offering his to mine, in turn. Weakly, I return his handshake, but I am totally gobsmacked. He is, to me, at thirteen, a love god extraordinaire: over six foot, slim and straight with neatly cropped brown hair (but not brilliantined like the Teddy Boy style, which I hate), hazel eyes and chiselled features, slick in a navy blazer jacket, shirt and tie.

'Nice to meet you, Paul,' I manage but then I lapse into silence. I am totally, overwhelmingly smitten. Until now, there has only been Elvis, a fantasy idol with looks and a voice that were created to arouse and excite the senses. This is the first time I've ever experienced physical attraction to someone in the real world. I am lost. I don't know how to behave, what to do. So, of course, I stay unusually mute. And I try not to stare at him, Mr Gorgeous, he who has instantly turned my world upside down.

Now Paul's mum and sister are bringing in the tea, biscuits, little homemade cakes specially baked for the occasion. And the women start to gossip, to enjoy themselves. Between mouthfuls, they run through a series of stories about their wartime years in Oxford Street, the girls they worked with, who'd run off with whom. (Most of their colleagues wound up in the arms of a free-spending GI, who vanished back to the States, leaving them holding the baby. Or, in one or two cases, having to explain the baby when hubby came home.) Dawn is fascinated by all of this, interrupting the women to ask questions. I've heard most of this stuff before. Paul looks at me, puts down his cup, smiles winningly and says, 'How's school going, Jacky? Mum says you go to a posh place called Skinners', isn't it?'

'Yeah,' I manage, desperate to impress, yet not knowing how to go about it. 'They call it Skinners' School for Snobs.

'The teachers are awful. They're posh but they're old. They only really like you if you're good at sport.'

Paul leans forward, still smiling. I've definitely got his attention.

'And are you good at sport?'

I shake my head. If I had any boy-catching skills, I'd simper now, smile engagingly. Or tell him what I am good at, English and history. But I have so much to learn and am so self-conscious, I just don't know how to talk to this eighteen-year-old who has commandeered my heart.

'No. I don't like it.'

'Never mind,' says Paul. 'We can't all be good at everything.'

And that is pretty much all we actually say to each other. Paul bids us a polite farewell as we're finishing our tea; he has to go out and meet a friend. And it is Dawn who shows me round their little terraced house, takes me out into the garden, asks me umpteen questions about London, what it's like, and says how she wants to come there one day.

I like her, probably because she's older, more grown-up – and, of course, she's His Sister, a link, a tie. Oh how I long to ask her about him, does he have a girlfriend? Would a nearly fourteen-year-old have a chance with him? Could I ever see him again? I discover that they do have a phone, a party line (a major frustration of the fifties, where people actually had to share their phone line with another household, though we always had our own line) and we swap numbers.

'I'll save up and come down to London!' she assures me as Molly and I say goodbye to them at the station.

But Dawn never does come to London. Nor do I ever see Paul again. Leicester, then, might as well have been another country. He was as remote and unattainable to me as Elvis, really. And I am left with my endless dreams and fantasies about a virtual stranger. What would happen if I got to meet him again? Would he like me? What would it be like to actually touch or kiss him? Such thoughts are usually accompanied by mental images of Paul and I, alone in his house, embracing passionately on their living-room sofa. I confide in no one about all this; I'm pretty sure my mum hasn't even picked up on my fixation with her friend's son. But hope still burns in my heart.

One evening, a few weeks later, the phone rings. My mum is in the bathroom, my dad still out working. It's Dawn. She's got a new, better job, yes Mum's OK, the Morris Minor's packed up, but Paul knows a man who can fix it. I take the plunge.

'How is Paul?' I venture.

'Oh he's fine. He liked you, Jacky,' she giggles.

'Really?'

I'm taken aback. I'm not expecting such wondrous news but my heart leaps, just the same.

'Yes, he told me not to say anything to Mum. He thought you were really pretty. He's definitely interested! I said, "Paul, you've got no chance, what with her being down in London with all those other boys."'

There are, of course, no other boys to speak of beyond my incessant reverie about her brother. But I don't give myself away. Vague promises are made, maybe I'll persuade my mum to get us up there again for another visit. But we never do hear any more from them – and I don't dare bring the subject up to Molly, for fear of betraying myself. In those days, of course, if someone rang and you were out, there were no answering machines or voicemails to take messages; people just had to keep trying until you were in.

So maybe there were more attempts to phone us. But the Paul-the-lover fantasy endures for quite a while. Until something quite different, but nonetheless disturbing, happens the following spring – and makes me understand just how little I know about the opposite sex.

Lolly and I are at Earl's Court, at the Ideal Home Exhibition. It's the school holidays and we've made the bus and tube journey here for our first-ever visit to the show. Someone has told us that you get lots of free food at the show, a real novelty for us and incentive enough to incite our curiosity – we certainly aren't there to look around at the interiors, way too aspirational for two Hackney fourteen-year-olds living in homes that are functional but hardly the stuff of gracious living.

And, sure enough, as we wander around the enormous space, we get to scoff the tiny samples, teeny sausages, small bits of white bread with dabs of sickly paste, as offered to us by smiling, attractive young women. We enjoy the delights of Getting Something For Free – we've never known anything like this before and, of course, it's an adults' world, a budding, emerging world of being able to buy what you want. And in our small way, without even being aware of it, we understand that we want all of this, choosing and buying, this is the future.

But there are other things we're not aware of. Wandering around, chattering, giggling loudly in that irritating, nigh-on hysterical way of young girls, reaching out excitedly to pick up the samples, we easily stand out among the largely adult crowd milling around. We are out of school uniform in neat little pleated skirts and blouses, carrying our precious wicker baskets. We think we look so grown-up. But anyone looking closely can see us for the school kids we are.

And someone does. Someone in the crowd is poised to pounce, watching us, two silly young girls, patiently waiting for their moment of opportunity. An unknown, faceless, devious pervert with a twisted mind has targeted us.

For when we leave the show and fish inside our baskets for

our purses and tickets home, we both discover a printed sheet, folded once, inside. It has been run off on a Banda (an early printer of sorts, where you wrote onto a special kind of carbon paper which was wrapped around a drum and run off to produce somewhat faintly printed copies, smelling of solvent).

And what we read on these printed sheets, slipped surreptitiously into our baskets without our noticing, reveals a shocking, overwhelming truth: someone, somewhere is getting off on the idea, the thought of us actually reading their filthy, provocative, quasi-pornographic questions, neatly typed in capitals, question after question about our bodies, our sexual awareness, our underwear, our parents, whether we masturbate, our toilet habits, nothing is missed.

Yet though it's a struggle for us, with our fairly limited knowledge when it comes to sex, we vaguely understand their purpose. We are, of course, stunned by this. Whatever little we knew about sexuality before, we know a bit more now. And it's very, very nasty. But such is our relative innocence that by the time we take our seats on the tube and make our way home, we're OK, though somewhat soiled by knowing we've brushed shoulders with something so awful. Yet what to do?

'Maybe we should show it to our parents?' asks Lolly, who is far less rebellious than I, much more conscious of doing the right thing.

'Nah, they'll only say it's our fault for going to the Ideal Home in the first place. And my dad would go potty,' I remind her, ever-conscious of the permanent state of war between me and Ginger and not wanting to even bring up the topic with my mum.

It doesn't occur to us to contact the police. Such was the semi-furtive, secretive nature of sex in those days, the idea of approaching a group of strangers with this dreadful anonymous document wouldn't even get a look in, one reason why this kind of sex pest could operate in the crowd in this way without fear of being caught.

'Look, let's just tear 'em up and chuck them in a bin,' I suggest.

And we do. Though of course, we cannot entirely forget the contents, their implication. Going 'all the way' sexually, in the jargon of the times, is still a long way away for us. But our naivety has been tarnished. And even though there is little consequence for us, the typed sheets aren't mentioned to anyone we know, even other girls at school.

But I do wonder what kind of harm those questions might have done to the minds of other kids back then when sex was still, for so many, such a taboo, unspoken topic? We wouldn't have been the only ones to get that printed sheet, after all…

CHAPTER 20
AN ENDING

School lunch break, sitting opposite the deserted netball pitch: me, Lolly and Brenda, whose parents run a sweet shop in Mare Street. We've just finished our school lunch, a mountain of gloppy mash, some watery carrots, an indefinable grey mess classified as 'mince' and, of course, the ubiquitous overcooked cabbage, virtually reduced to slime by the time it reaches our plates.

The others eat up but as usual, I cannot abide the mash and have developed a clever wheeze to avoid any attempt by nosy teachers to get me to clear my plate: whatever I don't like is surreptitiously scraped into a small brown paper bag, which then goes into my grey skirt pocket, where it often remains for days, until Molly decides to wash my things – and discovers the sickly, rotting mess.

Naturally, I consistently ignore her entreaties to stop this somewhat unhygienic habit.

'I can't stand the food, Mum, who cares if I don't eat it?' is the gist of my rationale.

Those lunches were the sole option, food-wise, in or around the school building. There were no vending machines, campus cafés or even handy corner shops to pop out to for sweets, crisps and fizzy drinks during school hours. Yet this afternoon, there's a development on that front: Brenda has started to pop modest supplies of Burton's Potato Puffs from her parents' stock into her schoolbag to sell at school for tuppence a bag. Lolly and I are the first of her lucky customers.

'Oooh they're gorgeous,' says Lolly, popping one of the delicate, round, air-filled puffs into her mouth.

'They sorta…melt in your mouth, don't they?'

'Mmm…' I agree, greedily popping the last handful from bag to mouth, savouring the last little scrunched-up bits, already wishing Brenda had brought more packets with her so I could stock up for the bus home.

'MUCH better than crisps, I reckon.'

Brenda is a quiet, pretty girl, never rude, and never in any kind of trouble. Yet this is quite an entrepreneurial feat for a fourteen-year-old.

After school, I quiz Lolly about it all, she knows Brenda quite well.

'Tuppence a bag is what they cost in the shop, why doesn't she sell them for less?'

'She can't. She has to give the money to her parents,' my friend explains.

My background, the world of duckers and divers, wheelers and dealers, is starting to show. I'd assumed she was nicking the goods, pocketing the cash. Now I can't, for the life of me, see the point of her endeavour. OK, we get to buy the puffs and that probably makes her more popular – but she doesn't make anything on it.

'Doesn't she mind, not getting anything out of it?'

'No, Jack. You don't understand, do you? Brenda's a good girl; she'd never do anything to upset her parents. She's not like you and me!'

Wise words. By now, our brief grammar school careers are jointly on the decline. Lolly's not as insolent or sarky as me. But she chatters incessantly, is always being sent out of class for this and, like me, hands in poorly finished work. Easily led, Lolly, the bright star of her family, has gradually started to follow me down the road to perdition. The teachers don't seem to dislike her as they do me: she's good at sport, especially netball, which counts for a great deal at Skinners'. I hate sport so much that I've taken to painting fake verrucas (warts) onto my feet and forging letters from home to get out of participating. Gradually, my influence results in Lolly bunking off sport too. And now, with my encouragement, we are occasionally sneaking out of school itself, after the afternoon register, changing out of our uniforms in the public toilet near the Regent Cinema and wandering off on the bus to Mare Street to hang around the shops.

Things are changing at home too. That December, around my fourteenth birthday, I'm through the front door from school to hear some unexpected news.

'The Old Man's had a stroke,' Molly tells me sadly.

'He was fine one minute, now he's in Barts. Your dad's with him now.'

I don't see my dad that night. I quickly fall asleep and in the morning wake up in time to hear the front door slam behind him. Molly fills me in.

'Ging is in a terrible state, Jac. It's touch and go with the Old Man. So you'd better be good. Don't do anything to upset him.'

Alas, within forty-eight hours it's all over for my grandfather. He's gone. Miriam is distraught; her sons whisk her away from the Lane for good and she is quickly ensconced with Neville's family, in his house in Mill Hill. We don't go to the funeral; kids didn't in those days anyway, and my mum, for some reason, opts to stay home to be with me when I get home from school.

Later, she tells me that a distraught Miriam tried to throw herself onto the coffin, giving a Command Performance. Ginger is subdued for a few days over Christmas, working on Boxing Day because there are race meetings, and for a short time, he comes home after work and goes straight to bed. I don't know what to say to him when I do see him; he's quiet and withdrawn. I'm shocked in one way, but I know that a turning point has been reached: my dad now runs the business alone.

Secretly, I'm relieved, of course, because there are no more enforced trips to Stoney Lane ahead. Though in one way, I liked my grandfather more than Miriam, I usually saw his benign, benevolent side and he was pretty generous with cash birthday gifts, and, on one occasion, he gave Ginger a pretty topaz and gold ring for me (still in my jewellery box but never valued).

But now he's gone, there's an embarrassingly acute lack of communication between me and my dad. The Old Man's demise is never discussed, never mentioned at all. But within a few weeks, the heavy boozing returns. It's around 10pm but

I'm wide awake in my bed, dreading the sound of the key in the lock as usual. I hear him come in, then there's a muffled silence for several minutes. Since this leaden, thick silence usually presages an explosion of shouting, I become unbearably tense, unable to relax or drift off to sleep. What is coming next?

What comes next is the sound of my father, wretched, distraught, sobbing his heart out, my mum desperately trying to comfort him. The loss of The Old Man has devastated him. I have never heard my father cry before. It is a pitiful sound.

'My poor father,' he sobs, barely coherent. My poor father. 'He liked the man that sold the hot peas…the hot peas…'

(I had no idea what he was going on about then, since hot-pea sellers had already vanished from London's streets but, of course, my grandfather, born in the late 1800s would have grown up with the sight and sound of men selling hot green peas in a round or oval tin on the streets in and around the Lane.)

But from then on, it is as if my father can no longer bear to live his life without a constant stream of booze. He was fairly consistently drunk before, with the occasional relatively sober few days in between. Now his heavy drinking, night after night, with only Sundays off, is relentless. And even the embarrassing, yet rowdily cheerful drunk who stood up to sing is gone. He drinks, comes home, is morose – and frequently belligerent.

The effect on me is dramatic. I can hear all the angry shouting, his outpourings of frustration at his friends, his family, the punters, from my tiny room. But I can't just lie there, waiting for it to stop, silently stuffing my fingers in my ears, trying my best to endure it as I've done in the past. Now, not yet a woman but not quite a child, I erupt in frenzied fury too. I run out into the hallway in my pyjamas, screaming at him.

'I HATE YOU, YOU BASTARD, WHY DON'T YOU SHUT UP, YOU'RE DRIVING US MAAAAD,' I scream.

This, of course, makes it all so much worse. There is absolutely no point in yelling like this at a very drunk person.

But I am so enraged by these hellish disturbances in our tiny space, and feel so trapped, so powerless, my only instinct as a means of taking control, getting it to stop, is to lash out. Fire meets fire.

It's truly awful. Ginger's drunken response to my outburst is to be hideously verbally abusive, frequently threatening to whack me for daring to challenge his authority – which he never does – but in truth, threatened physical abuse is still appalling. Having someone repeatedly tell you, 'You're not too old for me to belt you one, you little cow' sears your soul, demolishes your equilibrium. What a dreadful scenario. For we are both frustrated with the confines of our life, both trapped, unable to push out of our individual hells. And, of course, we share the famous Hyams temper, the cause of so many of his parents' eruptions. Talk about recipe for disaster.

My mum, as usual, is referee between us, desperately trying to stop the racket – easily heard throughout the flats, down the road – and ease the situation, calm things down.

But I scream out my frustration at her too.

'WHY DO YOU PUT UP WITH HIM?' I yell, when he finally disappears into the bedroom and passes out.

'HE MAKES ME SICK!'

Sometimes, it's so bad, he staggers out of the front door, giving us, at least, some relief from his presence. Then I go to bed, fall asleep and he creeps back, hours later, having partially sobered up and walked around the streets for hours.

Even now, I don't believe that this ongoing scenario, bad as it was, was directly responsible for my failure at school, my open scorn for authority. There were other factors. I was hypersensitive to what went on around me – but I wasn't a quiet, malleable child. I'd been spoilt rotten. I questioned everything – including our immediate surroundings, which, by now, were starting to trouble me: surely there were more pleasant places we could live? We could afford it, couldn't we? But it's clear now that what was happening to my dad was that he was scared silly without his support system. He'd loved his dad, looked up to him. And betting was a dodgy business in some ways. Yes, the bookies usually cleaned up. But you still needed your big cash wad, your front, your status in the local pecking order. And my dad already had a problem with serious responsibility, that's why it had suited him after the army to just take the easy money, stick to his dad.

Already a steady, heavy drinker, Ginger was bound to use booze even more to avoid confronting his fears. But, of course, it didn't work. That kind of over-the-top drinking never does. It creates more depression – which can only be quelled by a top up of alcohol. Mercifully, Molly's easy-going, get-on-with-it nature, did serve to calm things down somewhat. Till the next time…

But while the turbulence of my home life continues to wax

and wane, the months that follow my grandfather's demise, the end of one chapter in our lives, bring one or two less troublesome but nonetheless distracting events. Elvis goes into the US Army. His hair is shorn. Will this be the end, Lolly and I fret? Of course, as it always does, the surrounding hype and frenzy over this career milestone only serves to feed the collective hunger; Elvis was far from over, had only just begun. As for me, I too become in thrall to The Bottle.

Like most girls, I am not at all satisfied with what I have been given – thick light-brown hair with a natural curl. Increasingly conscious of how I look, I want a different look, a brighter, standout colour that makes me look more grown-up. So I embark on a bathroom experiment. Someone at school has told me that liquid peroxide can do amazing things to your hair, change the colour to blonde – all you need do is buy a bottle for a shilling or two from the chemist. This might sound a bit pathetic now. But there weren't too many hair products available in the shops then.

There was just one setting lotion available, called Amami, which gave you a temporary curl. You wet your hair with it before you set it, laboriously putting it in rollers secured with pins. If you had straight hair but yearned for a more permanent curly mop there was one type of home perm you could buy, the Toni with its memorable advertising campaign, 'Which twin has the Toni?'

This gave you a frizzy mess which everyone instantly knew was a home perm. It didn't look at all natural. In fact, it looked awful because the dampened curls, secured with pins, could only be effective if applied professionally. You couldn't do it yourself to get the desired effect. But because there was nothing else – other than the power of advertising – women went out in their millions and bought it.

Hair colouring was something else: for a start, obviously dyed hair was frowned upon, pretty much the mark of a loose woman. Girls risked scorn if their hair was dyed. It screamed: 'I'm a siren, come on you guys!'

It was the first-ever DIY over-the-counter home permanent hair colour, Miss Clairol, in the late fifties, that really started a shift in attitude ('Does she, or doesn't she? Only her hairdresser knows for sure' ran the ad campaign). Yet when I embarked on my first peroxide mission, any form of youthful hair dyeing was still largely viewed as A Naughty Thing. But who gave a fig for social mores?

My first attempt, at the tiny bathroom mirror, is a bit timid. I grab a lock of hair from the front, gingerly pour some peroxide onto cotton wool and furiously dab it onto my hair. Nothing happens (I have no idea you have to wait), so I take another lock from the front and dab on some more. Still nothing. And it stinks to high heaven. Maybe it doesn't work, after all. So I abandon the task.

The next day, of course, I see the result. Not a pretty sight. A sort of bright orangey brown – well... more orange, less brown. Still, it does work. So, over a period of weeks, with several bathroom sessions, I turn myself into a carrot top. Despite the orange effect, I mistakenly believe I look more sophisticated, more adult now. Ginger doesn't notice. Molly, of course, is not at all impressed with what I've done. But I've done my homework. I've discovered a photo of her in the forties. An avid follower of fashion, my mum's movie-star

Veronica Lake upswept Victory Roll hairstyle carried distinct blonde streaks at the front of her dark brown hair.

'Mum, did you dye your hair when I was little?' I'd asked innocently, before my visit to the chemist shop.

'Hmm…yes, Jac. It was all the rage then to look like Veronica Lake. So I did it with a bottle of peroxide. Took a while to grow out, mind you.'

Like mother, like daughter. Now, of course, my mum could indulge herself with a weekly shampoo-and-set at the salon on the corner of Kingsland Road. But I had my ammunition: when the air-raid sirens wailed and money was sparse, she too had taken to The Bottle.

So what could she say when I followed her lead?

CHAPTER 21
FIRST KISS

At long last, I have an admirer from the club. David is sixteen, lives in Clapton and goes to Grocer's, a grammar school, the local equivalent of Skinners'. He hangs around me like a little dog whenever I'm at the club, buying me soft drinks, making it quite obvious he has A Thing for Jacky.

But while I'm mightily reassured to find that I have some powers of attraction in my new kitten heels and seamless stockings, he's definitely not my type – shortish, skinny, pleasant enough but not exactly attractive, wavy hair, unremarkable, but always cheerful, with a smiley face.

There are two distinct types of boys on the Hill. The first were ordinary, working-class Jewish boys from the area like David, some with pushbikes – offering you a ride 'on the crossbar', of course, was an alternative to asking you to dance as a prelude to getting closer – though I always avoided this, since a pushbike ride usually went in the direction of Hackney Downs, the local courting spot, off limits unless you wanted to jeopardise your 'nice girl' status.

These boys were mostly quite aspirational, studying hard at grammar school, some the offspring of shopkeepers, market traders or tailoring workers, living locally in flats in rundown Victorian houses or on big council estates. You frequently hear about the grinding poverty of the East End (which was true to some extent), but, in fact, by the fifties huge numbers of people were continuously employed in the many clothing factories in and around Hackney and Stoke Newington, well into the seventies. Many of these boys wound up as accountants or cab drivers in and around the Essex suburbs, or West End retail managers, saving up every penny in order to run their own business. They weren't particularly stylish or sophisticated – their parents' means were modest – but these were the boys we were more or less expected to pair off with.

The other group were different, and mostly out of our league. They didn't hang out at the club; mostly they just hung around the Hill. They were much more sophisticated, sharply dressed Bad Boys, a few years older than us.

Lolly and I, our heads already turned by the smouldering sexual promise of the Ultimate Bad Boy (the man with the swivel hips across the Pond) found these boys more attractive, if dangerous. They openly looked for 'charver birds', girls who played fast and loose, willing to go all the way.

After school one day, while I stand at the bus stop, munching on a pickled cucumber, one of these sharp-suited Bad Boys, whom I know by sight but not by name, approaches me.

'How about it, two bob for a wank, yeah?'

I dive onto the stationary bus, shocked but laughing just the same. Upstairs, the risqué offer is an immediate topic of discussion with sisters Sylvie and Barbara, who have clambered up the stairs after me.

'Yeah I did that once,' says sullen Barbara, much to our amazement.

'Whaaat? You did it?' I say, mouth agape. Sylvie says nothing. She's silently hoping that this is just another one of her sister's sick jokes.

'Well I did it the once – but only half,' confides the enigmatic Barbara, leaving us even more baffled by this unfathomable statement.

Later, I ring Lolly and repeat the story. She is equally perplexed.

'Maybe she's just lying, you know what she's like…'

The Bad Boy at the bus stop was just chancing it, even if Barbara's story had some truth in it. But mostly these guys were flash types from more comfortably off families, some living in posher areas like Hendon, Golders Green or Hampstead, hanging out near the Hill because cute young Jewish girls congregated there. Some had fathers who had already started to make property fortunes (London's property boom started, low key, in the late forties as whole swathes of bombed-out areas started to change hands, to be developed decades later), while others ran successful retail businesses or factories.

Yet these slicker, more sophisticated boys with their winkle-pickers and Italian mohair suits with short, three-button jackets and narrow trousers, were out of our league for one very good reason: the kosher class divide. Hackney girls, like Lolly and myself, were sought after by these boys simply because we existed as attractive young teenagers. But neither their families nor ours expected us to form lasting relationships.

In late-fifties East London, everyone still had their place. Crossing the divide, from poorer working class to solid middle via a huge diamond engagement ring and a big 'do' in a West End hotel wasn't likely to be on the cards for us. The aspirational, hard-working Jewish families who had already 'made it' and moved out of the East End in the pre-war years to forge successful lives only wanted equally comfortably off partners for their kids. To these posher Jews, the fact that you still lived in Hackney marked you firmly within the ranks of the lower orders.

In fact, my mum had female cousins who having married up beyond their wildest dreams – from the poverty-stricken depths of Hessel Street, one of the East End's murkier quarters, to the leafy, quiet enclaves of Hampstead Garden Suburb – would not only ignore Molly's very existence but if closely questioned would immediately deny they'd ever even lived in the East End.

In my topsy-turvy world, of course, we lived like lords in a slum. I got whatever I wanted, when I asked for it. But I was firmly defined, on the social scale, by Hackney, the grim alleyway we lived in the mean streets of Dalston Junction. This class divide didn't bother Lolly and I at this stage, I might add. We were too young to give it much thought. But we certainly understood it, were conscious of it.

In my last year at Skinners' I develop an intense fascination with a posh good-looking Hill boy called Stephen, quite short, brown eyed and part of a group of Bad Boys with very dodgy reputations led by a non-Jewish boy, Richard

Longthorpe, an early Mod ringleader. All are snazzy dressers: sharp Italian mohair suits with narrow lapels, button-down shirts from Cecil Gee, pointed-toe winkle-pickers, handmade in a shop down the Lane.

In fact, Mod fashion, which only really got going commercially later, in the sixties, is reputed to have kicked off via such Jewish middle-class groups like these. And as schoolgirls, Lolly and I already admired this 'cool' style of dressing. It appealed to us. We weren't keen on the slicked back hair, jeans and leather jacket biker look. So Stephen, a cool dresser and looker if ever there was one, is top of my hit list. But beyond the odd hello or glance, it never goes any further. We don't even know where he lives.

Then comes a window of opportunity. I discover, a week or so in advance, that Molly and Ginger are going out to a big bash, a West End party with some of my dad's punters. The details are vague but they'll be gone for several hours, leaving me, they innocently believe, home alone.

What this means to me is, joy of joys, I can throw my own 'evening in', as they were known. Essentially an evening in was a group of kids going round to someone's empty house or flat, pairing off, and mostly snogging with the lights out. How far it all went beyond that depended on the willingness of the girl to move things along; at that stage, it probably did move sometimes into 'heavy petting' territory. But only sometimes.

With some careful plotting, Lolly and I let it be known around the club that Jacky will be hosting an evening in. All are welcome. This, I hope, will be my Big Chance with Stephen: the invite has been issued all along the Hill.

About a dozen young girls and boys crowd into my cramped

flat that evening and start to pair off. The beautiful Stephen actually turns up, climbs the smelly stone stairs in his immaculate Italian suit and steps into my home. Oh joy. Yet he and Richard Longthorpe take one look around at the snogging couples on armchairs and sofa – and promptly leg it. David, who'd turned up earlier and is still interested, is waiting for his moment and decides to pounce.

'Come outside to the balcony,' he begs me. So I do, disappointed by my dashed dreams of Stephen but now open to experience, at least.

And there, on the dingy balcony of our flats, I have my first-ever kiss. It's all a bit slippery, no tongues deployed yet, but we keep going with mutual enthusiasm. This was it, 'necking' they called it (no one had ever heard of the word foreplay). And while I'm pretty indifferent to David generally, I find I quite like being in his embrace: it feels grown-up.

But not for long. In the time-honoured tradition of such events, a big shock: Molly and Ginger trundling up the stairs to our flat hours before they're expected. The door to their home ajar, they are appalled to step inside to find two couples snogging fervently on the couch and other pairs doing likewise on chairs and armchairs. Luckily, no one has attempted to raid Ginger's cocktail cabinet for the booze; there hasn't been enough time. But me, I am caught bang to rights, in the embrace of David, who moves like lightning down the stairs and away into the Dalston night the minute my parents appear on the scene.

David's vanishing act doesn't upset me. Essentially, the whole exercise has been purely experimental; I've long been desperate to know what it's like to snog a boy. For my parents, of course, this scenario is proof positive that their daughter is on the road to ruin.

Need I say that Ginger, who isn't, for some reason, in his usual pissed-as-a-fart state tonight, merely a bit tiddly, goes ballistic? Everything relating to my new teenage world is scheduled to be banned, my nylons, my hoop skirt – the late fifties were the era of full skirts and taffeta petticoats – my Elvis records (which is daft because I can always go to Lolly's flat to listen to hers). Even Lolly is mooted for the banned list. My dad has recently taken an avid dislike to Lolly's mum, Fay, though he's never met her face-to-face, only spoken to her briefly on the phone.

'She's a tart,' he'd fumed to my mum.

Fay loved bingo and went out regularly to play locally. With a cabbie husband working nights, this, according to my dad, showed she was a bad mother. And, of course, in his macho view, this also confirmed her status as a sleep-around gal. And now, of course, my balcony snog has given him ammunition to ban Lolly and her family from my life.

'You're not seeing that Lolly, either! She's a little tart too, a bloody bad influence.'

(The truth was the other way round, of course.)

'What do you bloody know, all you do is get pissed you bastard!' is my standard response.

The bedroom door slams. I fall onto my bed, disappointed and embarrassed at being caught, angry at my dad's typical over-reaction. But part of me, nonetheless, feels a bridge has been crossed: at least I'm now a Snogee.

For about a week after the aborted evening in I am grounded: I go to school, come home, eat my dinner in my room – and stay there. David, apparently, is still keen, undaunted by the spectre of an irate Ginger, which says much for his youthful ardour. But alas, for David, I am lost to him: my experiment over, my dad's attempts to limit my life soon forgotten, I am in no way ready for a steady situation with a Nice Boy. Oh no. I want something different, more exciting than a rather scruffy Stamford Hill Club boy.

'He's not exactly nice looking,' I remind Lolly as we munch away on our lunchtime bag of potato puffs. 'And I can't stand that big jumper he wears, it looks like his mum knitted it and lost the pattern.

'Anyway, he's got a big nose, he looks SO Jewish…'

How superficial can you be? Instead of appreciating David's loyalty after the embarrassing denouement, the shape of his nose and his baggy knit are sufficient to consign him to the rubbish heap. He takes it well, stops hanging around me and quickly moves on to another girl from the club who goes to Laura Place school. Recently I learned that he became a highly successful multi-millionaire businessman. Who would have known it, eh?

Lolly, too, is starting to conduct her own youthful experiments around this time. And we learn a valuable lesson from what happens next: 'Loose Talk Costs Lives' proclaimed the posters plastered all over the country during the war years. In this case, of course, lives were not imperilled. But Lolly's reputation around the Hill is about to take a bit of a nosedive via some serious blabbing.

Lolly has long had a suppressed passion for a boy called Malcolm. He lives near Hackney Downs in the same block of flats as Lolly's grandparents. She visits her grandparents regularly, so this gives Lolly ample time and opportunity to smile encouragingly at Malcolm, who is exceptionally good looking and, at sixteen, already something of a Hackney heartbreaker. One girl in our year, Susan, has already set her sights firmly on Malcolm and they've been an item for a while, so Lolly has kept very quiet about fancying him like mad.

One summer evening, as Lolly leaves her grandparents' flat, she finds Malcolm at the bottom of the stairs, leaning on his pushbike and flashing her a come-hither grin. Two of his mates are with him: Don, another good-looking local boy, and a fat boy called 'Buddy', nicknamed because he wears big black-framed glasses à la Buddy Holly.

'Goin' home, Lolly?' coos Malcolm the Charmer, who knows the estate where Lolly lives about a mile or so away.

Lolly nods, afraid to say much. This is the closest she's ever got to Malcolm. But she's heard through the Skinners' grapevine that he and Susan aren't courting right now. They're having 'a break'.

Throwing caution to the winds, she says its OK for the trio, pushing their bikes along the pavement, to accompany her home. Yet minutes into their stroll, Malcolm seizes the initiative.

'Look, we can cut across the Downs here and get there quicker,' he tells Lolly, a signal to his mates to leg it, buzz off. Which they promptly do.

Lolly knows perfectly well she should now make some excuse and walk off, get away from the Downs. But this doesn't happen. A few minutes later, they're sitting on the Downs, Lolly chattering away nonstop to cover her nerves.

'Everyone says that Skinners' girls are snobs,' she prattles.

'You can't be a snob if you live in council flats, can you?'

Malcolm doesn't answer. He just smiles beguilingly – and promptly grabs Lolly for a kiss. She does not pull away. She's been kissed before by a boy she didn't like much. This is Malcolm! Much more exciting. More kisses.

'This is niiice,' thinks Lolly dreamily.

Then, predictably, Malcolm lunges and tries to grab Lolly's boobs. She is quick to push him away. She knows she's already in trouble for going on the Downs and just necking with Someone Else's Baby. Anything else is unthinkable.

Malcolm jumps up. He can't be bothered to try again.

'Come on, let's walk you home, I'll be late for tea.'

Silently they trudge all the way back to Lolly's estate. He says goodbye without attempting another kiss.

Lolly doesn't tell a soul about what has happened, not even me. But within a day or so, the news is out: Gallant Malcolm, so handsome, so treacherous, has delightedly rushed back to his mates to boast: Yeah, he went on the Downs with Lolly who then, shamelessly, let him unhook her bra.

'That Lolly's a right goer,' he tells them.

'Reckon she'd probably go all the way if you wanted…'

It's both unfair and cruel. The lie spreads around the Hill, all the way to Skinners' and the ears of Susan, who confronts Lolly after class.

'I hear you've been after Malcolm,' she sneers bitchily.

'So what?' says Lolly shakily, attempting a defiance she doesn't really have.

'Malcolm's not interested in little TARTS,' she hurls at a crestfallen Lolly, who soon gets the full story of what Malcolm has been saying from one of the other girls.

Lolly is shocked and bewildered. She doesn't deserve this. In one fell swoop devious, two-timing Malcolm has somehow cleared himself with his beloved. And upped the ante as a Lothario with his mates. Now, whenever she runs into Susan and her gang, there are bitchy whispers and gales of spiteful laughter. Who can underestimate the cruelty of young girls? Or the perfidious behaviour of young men?

But if our random experiments with boys are taking up much of our time and energy, our school careers are now in freefall. After-hours detention is now *de rigeur*, as are summons to the headmistress, Miss Gray, for a talking-to. On one memorable if shameful occasion, Lolly and I wind up in detention together – and spend an entire half hour standing before the teacher, giggling incessantly. It's all so hilarious for us. We look at each other, that makes us giggle. We look at the teacher, more fuel for snickering. It's outrageous – and also a bit tragic. Because it is crystal clear to the teachers that it's a waste of time trying to teach girls like us. Time to talk to The Parents.

Molly and Ginger are invited to a session at the school with the headmistress. They dress to the nines, as usual, my dad, unbelievably sober in his new Savile Row tailored 'whistle', white neatly pressed shirt and silk patterned tie. Molly dons her new yellow wool jigger coat, a loose three-quarter-length style very popular in the fifties. Miss Gray, however, is not interested in presentation. Their daughter, she explains, is a hair's breadth away from expulsion. She is bright but she doesn't study at all, and her insolent attitude is disrupting the class. What do they have to say?

There have already been heated discussions at home. Lolly's

family are clubbing together to pay to send her to secretarial school so she can leave Skinners' after turning fifteen and learn shorthand and typing. I, of course, demand this too. It means several months more of study – then out into the world, a job, earning money. Freedom. As usual, my parents are caving in to me. Anything for a quiet life.

'We think if she goes to secretarial school when she's fifteen, there's quite good opportunities for her, there's a big demand for office workers and secretaries,' explains Ginger.

'And the money's very good.'

He's right, in a way. Better a teenage typist, earning money, than a reluctant stroppy schoolgirl, wreaking havoc, ignoring her studies.

'Yes, but it's not the same as the sort of career she could have if she worked hard and studied,' sighs Miss Gray. 'The money might be good now. But it will never really go up.'

What she means, of course, is that study, 'A' levels and university could lead to a Civil Service career, or teaching – where salaries, plus pensions would climb, albeit slowly.

None of this is likely to mean much to my parents. But they somehow respect Miss Gray's quiet authority and her words are mulled over afterwards.

'It's funny she said that about the money, Ging. How does she know?' mused Molly.

'Dunno. I reckon she has to say that, anyway. Can't be seen to encourage people to let their kids out at fifteen, can she?'

I am fortunate that Ginger's wad of readies can easily be deployed to fork out the twenty-two guineas per term it will cost to send me to Pitmans College in Southampton Row for a year. Though at the time, of course, I don't fully perceive this: it's just another thing I have to have because a) I hate Skinners' and any attempt by authority to regulate my behaviour, and b) my friend is doing it, so it's a must-have.

But the Pitmans decision, unbeknown to all of us, carried with it a huge advantage for me down the line. For while shorthand and touch-typing were the prerequisites to a secretarial route back then, they could also prove to be very valuable tools for anyone wishing to work as a journalist. None of us, of course, had any idea that my path would eventually lead to a lifetime in journalism. But this time, the spoilt child who stamped her foot and yelled until she got her way had unwittingly hit upon something of lasting value.

Although all that was a long, long way ahead…

CHAPTER 22
THE APPRENTICE

The sixties dawned. By the end of 1960, Elvis was out of the army, growing his hair and warning us: It's Now or Never. And in a way, he was right; who imagined we were heading into the definitive post-war decade of explosive social change?

For me, the era began by saying farewell to school, an unmemorable transition. I just left class, as usual, bundled all my stuff into a carrier bag, and waited impatiently at the bus stop opposite the hated Victorian building, the scene of my Great Failure, to board the 649 bus home. There was no ceremony, no real sense of moving on to pastures new, other than briefly saying goodbye to my cronies. (No teacher had much to say to me.)

Lolly had already left a month or so before. A few girls were openly envious of our freedom but most were quite sniffy about it all: it was no secret that expulsion would have been my fate had my parents not pre-empted the authorities by pulling me out.

So just a week after departing school, I stood, in my little grey-and-white Prince of Wales check suit with its below-the-knee-length straight skirt, topped with my lemon Orlon cardigan and short boxy jacket, waiting for another bus going in a totally different direction: towards the West End.

The 38 bus runs from Dalston Junction, down Balls Pond Road and through Islington, all the way down Rosebery Avenue and along Theobald's Road to the corner of Southampton Row, where Pitmans College stood.

My life was changing for ever, yet in Dalston itself very little had changed on the surface: Ridley Road was still crowded, dirty and scruffy, the High Street shops still dingy if a bit more well stocked with consumer durables, and Kingsland Road jammed with people who looked a tad brighter, less downtrodden and no longer quite so lean and hungry. The Wimpy Bar was virtually full most days; Cooks Pie & Eel shop, with the wriggling, slimy eels in full view in the front window, did a continuous roaring trade.

Yet if you looked again, the place still bore the scars of the old air-raid and ration-book existence. Many bombsites around Shacklewell Lane remained untouched, merely boarded up. The timberyard opposite our flat was noisily going full tilt. Maisie and son remained, eking out their existence in their hideout. The boys in the car yard still ran out to offer Molly help with her shopping bags. An Irish family in a first-floor flat below moved out, back to Ireland, to be replaced by some friends of theirs, another Irish couple without kids. The rebuilding and re-branding of whole swathes of East London into more fashionable, trendy areas was still decades off. But my dad's bookie world was changing dramatically.

Street betting was poised to go straight. In 1960, the government announced that within a year, betting shops would be legalised. My dad's semi-illegal business could now be 100 per cent legit. There'd be no more bungs or grateful rounds in the pub to friendly coppers. More canny operators would have seen this demise of the bung as a real advantage. Not my dad; for him, all the change meant was that the Middlesex Street premises could be vacated. Just around the corner, in Harrow Place, the Hyams name could now be hoisted above a fully fledged betting shop, complete with counter clerk and blackboard with betting prices scrawled in chalk, for all to see, not just the lucky sods with phones who could afford to run an account.

The Day of the Runner was ending; the street corner and public house furtive exchange of betting slips was over. No more newspaper court reports that this or that hapless runner had been formally charged for 'loitering on the streets for settling bets' and fined a tenner.

Now, because the people's passion for betting was clearly an ingrained national pastime, it was a no-brainer for the government to start to clean up, legally, on the betting front: for a canny bookie, the post-war betting bonanza was now a route to greater riches. Or in Ginger's case, it should have been…

Why he decided to acquire a partner in his new venture was never clear. After all, the business itself was well established around the Lane. Maybe with his dad gone, he needed the backup of someone with serious cash. In any event, the new partner, a pale, skinny man called Leslie, came on board to help fund my dad's new venture as a legal betting-shop owner. He'd be a sleeping partner only.

'It's gonna be the first-ever betting shop in the City of London area,' Ginger told everyone proudly.

Well…a distinction of sorts, I guess. Ginger loved the City: bomb scarred as it still was he regarded it as his territory, a significant and fascinating area, a historical landmark of London's early beginnings. And now we no longer had to make those horrible Sunday treks to the Lane – there were never any enforced visits to my grandmother, now in the suburbs, since most of my dad's parental affection had been reserved for his father – I started to understand for myself the City's fascination after a trip to The Monument, climbing the hundreds of stairs right to the top, to gaze down on the vast city streets below. At fifteen, out of school, new and different vistas of London were starting to open up for me – far beyond the mundane confines of Dalston and the Hill.

In a way, Pitmans was a significant halfway house between my home life and my subsequent working life in and around the West End. The college was a bustling, busy place with all types of students of both sexes, charging up and down the stairs, racing to be on time for classes, all determined to pick up the rudiments of office skills and finding a niche in the now developing commercial world. Why did boys want to learn to type? Lolly and I wondered. Surely they didn't want to be shorthand typists, like us? (Mostly, they didn't, they were hoping to be journalists.) And how come every single day was so crammed? We had shorthand and typing classes twice each day, interspersed with French lessons; we'd already done French at Skinners' so it made up the curriculum. And, of course, it had been impressed upon us at home that this could not, in any way, be a repeat of

Skinners'. There'd be no slacking, no skiving off to the Hill to giggle and munch on pickled cucumbers. We were there to learn important skills that would deliver us into the working world and earn us good money. Our parents were paying: we'd better get cracking.

'Monty says he wants to see me earning in six months' time,' Lolly told me, nervous at the unknown hurdles facing us. I hadn't been told this in so many words but I was a bit daunted at first too. Ginger was preoccupied with sorting out the new shop, getting everything shipshape, my mum holding her breath, hoping against hope that me going out to work would mark the end of the war between me and my dad (she was seriously wrong, alas).

But incredibly, we did get stuck in, learning to touch type with a big metal cover concealing the keys to the big Royal or Remington typewriter – something I struggled with at first but eventually just about got the hang of – and gradually unravelling the huge mystery of learning to write Pitman shorthand. The whole point of the intensive learning schedule was to keep you slugging away at it, day in, day out, until you got up to speed. And it worked. After a few months of not having a clue what the innumerable shorthand squiggles, pee, bee, tee, dee, chay, some strokes light, some heavy, really represented, one day a little light clicked on in my head and I 'got' what shorthand was all about: a phonetic representation of the English language. It all started to flow. In fact my shorthand was better than my typing. I wasn't nimble fingered at the keyboard. Even when you had some idea of what you were doing, typing by touch alone, clattering away (it was a very noisy business, with thirty or so students tapping away on manual typewriters, hour in, hour out), you had to get up to a decent speed to get your leaving certificate. Employers wanted shorthand typists who could type quickly, spell properly and take down shorthand dictation at a good speed, say eighty words a minute.

The big carrot for all this frenzied activity was the prospect of a choice of office jobs galore in London for kids like us, even though we hadn't completed our education. Such was the volume of demand, businesses big or small had to compete like mad for competent people: hence the clamour for Pitmans skills, the growing number of employment agencies like Brook Street Bureau and the slow and steady emergence of 'The Temp'.

Eight pounds a week plus luncheon vouchers for a junior shorthand typist in London's West End sounds very modest now – but for a fifteen-year-old then it meant real consumer power, new clothes on tap, sharply pointed-toe brown stilettos from Dolcis at £5 a pair. Lolly and I, already eager shoppers with our parents' money, couldn't wait to have our own cash: and we were not alone, part of a huge economic wave giving birth to a spending boom spearheaded by youngsters: we, not our parents, who'd struggled through war going without, would never have it so good.

Day after day, we plodded away at the typewriters, took down fake business letters in our wonky shorthand, listened intently as the formally worded documents were dictated to us over and over again. 'Dear Sir. With reference to your letter of the twenty fourth…we remain, yours respectfully, and so on… It was dull, repetitive and frequently it seemed endless; you never thought you'd get there. But we did. Despite the somewhat disturbing behaviour of one of the typing supervisors, a nun called Sister Brigid who would regularly get behind your chair and literally shove the chair forwards, sadistically propelling you towards the covered keyboard if she felt you were inattentive or losing momentum. Sister Brigid was a bully. There was no doubt of that. But she had no time for the protracted 'Stand Creature' scenes of student humiliation that took place at my last school. You just copped it. Your mum and dad were paying. There was no other option but to keep clattering away.

It's a Sunday night and I'm at an 'evening in' with a new swain, a boy of seventeen called Andy whom I know from the club. Andy is great: tall, blond, attractive and bright, he's already poised to go to university, a notch up from the likes of Dopey Stephen whom I'd previously paired off with at another 'evening in' only to discover that the object of my passion is a rubbish, sloppy kisser – and a bit wooden, a conversational duffer. He looks good, dresses sharp. But that's it. He has nothing else to offer.

Andy is a much better bet; he's knowledgeable and interesting. Necking with him is great, the real deal. He never attempts to fumble with my bra or go any further. And he's funny.

I'm sitting cosily on his lap in a big flat in Stamford Hill; the adults living here are out, and around us are other couples all furiously snogging like mad.

'See that girl over there?' Andy whispers, nuzzling my neck, pointing to a girl draped over a happy youth on the opposite chair.

'She'll make a good grandmother.'

'How d'ya know?' I wonder, marvelling at his perspicacity. After all, he's pointing to a not particularly pretty, straggly-haired plump girl from Clapton Pond.

'Aah, that's my secret,' he teases, reaching out for another lingering kiss.

I don't dare ask him what my prospects are for good grandmotherhood. I'd be mortified if he said he thought I was a strong contender. Though most of the girls I know are already openly discussing engagements and white-frocked nuptials, the housewife-cum-mother role and all it entails has not taken shape on my horizon. I know it should, of course, given the amount of time and mental energy that goes into boy chasing, speculating on their attributes and now, finally, dating local boys like Andy. But, for me, I know there is too much going on out there in the world for me to experience to fasten firm onto this idea of wife, mother…let alone granny.

What he meant, of course, was that nearly all the girls in our world would have been devastated not to be married off with kids on the way within the next few years. Being a childless spinster to my contemporaries meant shame, no one wanted you. (It was equally bad to be an unmarried mum, trapped by nature's whim but a social pariah nonetheless.) Being a granny was seen as the crowning achievement in family life. Having an interesting career, being financially independent and maybe then thinking about choosing a partner – or having kids – was still a long way off as a normal option for young women. Andy, more perceptive than most, saw it all clearly.

Yet that was our last encounter, our final necking session. Within weeks he'd gone off to university in the Midlands. I then discovered he was already spoken for: a green-eyed blonde girl from Guildford, already at university. I mourned him briefly: for about two weeks. But that passing comment made an impact on me: at fifteen, it helped me understand more about myself, that my horizons were quite different from those around me.

Life at home was changing somewhat for me because I saw little of my dad, unless I was still awake at night to hear him come in. I was out on the bus to Southampton Row before he rose, and on weekends I mostly slept through the day, a teenage pattern that became a routine until the time I left home. Usually, in winter, I'd sleep through weekend mornings, only stirring to eat – a Sunday lunch of roast beef and Yorkshire pudding was usually taken, sitting up in my bed – then I'd dive out, plonk the plate in the kitchen sink and go back to sleep. Until it was time to go out, get ready, meet Lolly. Or go on the odd date.

After the David incident, of course, my dad's attitude to my developing social life worsened. I was growing up, moving towards some sort of independence. Now the rows and explosions were no longer about dragging The Unwilling Daughter to family visits – instead, there was a ludicrous possessiveness about me and the opposite sex.

I never suggested that any boy that liked me come to the flat; I'd arrange to meet them elsewhere. Often they'd already have a taste of Ginger's temper if they rang me at home. If I was out and he picked up, he'd yell abuse at them, tell them to eff off and slam the phone down. Sometimes the baffled recipient would tell me about this. Embarrassed, I'd just mumble something and quickly change the subject. I never ever wanted to discuss any of this stuff. Even Lolly, who knew how it was for me with my dad, chose to ring when she knew I'd pick up. But even she wasn't fully aware of how frequently my dad was plastered. Or abusive.

One Sunday night, not long before I leave Pitmans, I'm out with a Hill boy called Stan: tall, dark, handsome – but mostly silent. Conversation with Stan is minimal. He's so good-looking, a real hunk, and I don't really understand that it's actually shyness that keeps him so quiet. We've gone to the cinema at Stamford Hill to see *Psycho*, which has managed to scare the life out of me – and Stan has attempted a tentative bit of hand-holding – a sign of life at least! – but nothing more. Afterwards, Silent Stan accompanies me, still saying very little, on the bus to Shacklewell Lane – and offers to walk me to my door.

I can hardly refuse, though I know my dad might be home as it's Sunday night. Worse, it's now well past my curfew time, 10pm, when we eventually get off the bus and stroll down Shacklewell Lane, hand-in-hand, towards my street.

Oh no. It can't be happening. A furious Ginger, enraged that I'm still out, already suspecting A Boy is involved, is standing on the corner of our street. He's not visibly drunk. But he's steaming with suppressed anger.

'Whaddya think you're doin' you little cow?' he yells.

Before I can respond, he walks up to me – and promptly slaps me across the face.

It's a devastating shock, your dad whacking you like this in front of a boy. I'm not really hurt. Just humiliated beyond belief.

'Sorry, sorry – er Mr Hyams,' says Stan, stumbling, incoherent, clueless as to how to react. At well over six foot –

he towers over my dad – you might expect him to stand his ground, defend me. It's all perfectly innocent. But he's far too intimidated by my dad's rage, his hideous invective.

'Get outta here you cow's son before I kick you up the ass!' he bellows at the rapidly departing Stan. Then, damage done, he turns and stomps off in the opposite direction, knowing damn well he's gone too far this time.

Sobbing with shame and rage, I stumble down the street, up to our flat, banging at the door-knocker like crazy. My mum, already expecting trouble, is nonetheless shocked at my state.

'He bloody hit me!' I scream at her.

'That bastard hit me! I hate his fucking guts! I HATE HIM!'

My mum hugs me close, does her level best to calm me. Distressed at what has happened, she is nonetheless powerless to control my dad's over-the-top behaviour.

'I'm sorry, Jac, I'm sorry I gave you such a rotten dad,' she tells me.

'SO WHY DO YOU STAY WITH HIM? WHY DON'T YOU GO?' I scream.

We've been here before: this pokey, noisy place, the boozing, the unreasonable rages, my constant feeling of being stifled, hemmed in. But we both know the answer. My dad earns 'a good living'. He reminds us of this frequently in the midst of his angry tirades, with his perpetual mantra: 'I work my balls off for you, you have the finest and the best' and so on. So without any sort of economic freedom from our dependence on this 'good living' where would we go, how could we survive?

This is the only time my dad displays any physical violence towards me, though heaven knows he's threatened it often enough in outbursts. So bad has it been between us lately, my mum, trapped fast in the midst of our stormy natures, had even resorted to leaving me a begging note on my bed a few weeks before.

'Please be a good girl, Jac,' the note said. 'It would be so much easier for us if you didn't keep rowing with your dad.'

How desperate must she have been to see an end to this constant turmoil, the regular ding-dongs, the shouting, yelling and screaming that punctuated our lives so frequently. I never forgot that pleading little note. Yet at the time, of course, I ignored her plea: the callous teenage tyrant who only cares about her own needs, her own wants; undisciplined emotionally, I don't know how to stop myself reacting to his behaviour, his very presence in our lives. But I vow, there and then, that if he ever does anything like this again, I will flee, run away, no matter what. I'll go to Lolly. I'll find a way to get away from this somehow...

Finally, I cry myself into sleep, exhausted by my frustration at our lot. I have no idea what time my dad creeps back, ashamed, into the flat. There's no apology, just a few days of relative calm. As for Silent Stan, he never phones me again. I'm not surprised. But now I have something to hang onto: very soon, at least, I'll have my own money from work – and be out, spending as much time as possible away from this place. Escape will be my salvation.

Only I don't quite understand exactly how long that's going to take.

CHAPTER 23

PARTY WITH THE KRAY TWINS

It is white, tight and made from beautiful guipure lace. It has a shiny satin band round the waist and thin satin spaghetti straps, a figure-hugging sheath dress to knock 'em in the aisles, the sort of dress that Marilyn Monroe wore. My mum, champagne glass aloft, teetering on her high-heeled silver sandals, postures and preens in front of the living-room mirror.

She's had the dress made to measure, as usual. She looks like a pocket Venus: it shows off her slim, flat hips and full bust to perfection. And tonight is the debut of the lace dress, its first ever outing. A party, in posh Knightsbridge at a place called Esmeralda's Barn, to celebrate the acquittal of Ronnie and Reggie Kray, the East End's most famous sons. Yet again, for the umpteenth time, the naughty Twins have wriggled out of trouble; charged this time with 'loitering with intent' to steal parked cars in Hackney, they hired a top female barrister to defend them. And wouldn't you know it, the court has dismissed the charges. Krays: 1. Coppers: Zilch.

'Whaddya think, Ginger?' says Molly, twirling round,

fishing for compliments as usual, knowing full well she looks fabulous. The lace alone, sourced from a pricey West End fabric emporium, has cost my dad a wad of notes, let alone the cost of getting it made.

'Fantastic, Mol, fantastic,' says my dad, grinning, opening his cherished cocktail cabinet and pouring himself a pre-party double.

'The boys've invited all sorts of people this time, film stars, posh people, you name it. It's gonna be a really big night.'

I'm not really interested in all this – but I do like my mum's taste in dresses; it's bang up-to-the-minute fashionable, even better than the white tasselled sheath with diamanté straps also hanging in her ever-crowded wardrobe.

I'm desperate for them to go out and party because it means the luxury of having the flat – or rather, the phone – to myself for a few hours, rather than having to duck down to the draughty phone box on the little roundabout in Shacklewell Lane for one of my lengthy phone calls to my friends. By now, I'm at that stage where I don't want my phone conversations overheard, so the freedom of the flat tonight is a bonus for me.

As a child, of course, my folks would often use the services of Renee, a teenage babysitter who lived round the corner in the Arcola Street council flats. She loved babysitting for us, mainly because my dad, typically, was over-lavish with the 'bonuses' that usually came along with her hourly rates.

'Treat yourself, gel,' he'd say, pissed as a newt, stuffing an extra ten-shilling note into her hand on arriving home. What an easy gig. All she had to do was get me into my pyjamas and bed. Then she'd plonk herself down on the couch, tune into the radio, listen to the *Billy Cotton Band Show* or, on Sundays, *Sing Something Simple*, knit, and plan what she'd do with my dad's bonus.

I'm aware, of course, that they are partying with two of the East End's most celebrated, notorious crims. My dad's relationship with the Twins has spanned many years. He'd first known them as teenagers when they'd worked on their grandad's stall on Petticoat Lane. And he'd watched them, at eighteen, when they boxed professionally at the Royal Albert Hall with their older brother, Charlie.

'The twins were good little boxers,' he'd recall wistfully, as if a totally different kind of career had merely been snatched from them by a cruel twist of fate. He knew their dad, Charlie, quite well too; like my dad, Charlie had worked 'on the knocker' flogging clothing and buying gold and silver from door-to-door all over England. He was also a heavy gambler. And a serious drinker.

The twins, however, didn't think much of their dad, in complete contrast to their relationship with their mum, Violet, whom they worshipped. They were known to be very respectful towards women generally. Yet it was also common knowledge around the manor that they'd been known to beat their father up. Rumour had it that on one occasion, they'd hung him upside down, from a fourth-floor window, repeatedly threatening to let him go. In the pub afterwards, Charlie, however, wasn't in the least bit nonplussed about this, telling people like my dad exactly what had gone down.

This violence, of course, was pretty much par for the course in their East-End world. And my dad had grown up amidst it. Men went to the pub, fought each other sometimes, went home and, in some cases, beat their kids – or the missus. Women stoically put up with it, mostly for economic reasons – changes to the divorce laws were decades away. And, of course, the law didn't fully recognise domestic violence then. It was just something that happened. Frequently.

But despite his origins and his love of the bottle, my dad never attempted to hit my mum, even when frustration and anger overwhelmed him later in life. OK, the furious verbal exchanges when he was badly drunk demonstrated a violent aspect of his life, surely the same kind of abuse he'd heard as a kid. The language was certainly coarse, ugly. But I never saw any punch-ups, men fighting each other, as a child. The violence and intimidation that was the darker side of the criminal East End world was around us, but me and my mum didn't get to see it.

To my parents, the Kray Twins were part and parcel of the East End world, usually a focal point for gossip and stories about their exploits; by the sixties, a kind of seedy glamour was attached to actually knowing them. The twins admired Ginger. Because my dad was known around the Lane to be a whizz with figures and a bit of a scribe and skilled letter writer, one day a youthful Ronnie had turned up at my dad's office with a special request.

'Can ya write us a letter, Ginger, to the court?' he'd asked, wanting a carefully worded testimonial to be read out in court, a common practice at the time. Literacy was not the Twins' strong point and truth, of course, had a way of disappearing whenever they wanted to make a point.

My dad complied. He more or less had to do it. Even then, long before their crimes got completely out of control, few in the Lane refused the Krays a favour. And they, in turn, never forgot if you'd helped them out. Which was a double-edged sword, because there was always a chance they'd ask you again. And again.

In the late fifties, when their firm was on the rise, the Krays had even invited my dad to leave the bookie business and join their coterie of hangers-on. By then, illegal gambling was really popular; it was known that legalisation wasn't far off, so there'd been heavy investment in gambling clubs and casinos. Ginger, they thought, with his betting nous and literary skills, might be useful. He could go on the twins' payroll, couldn't he?

'We'll see that the missus and the little 'un are looked after, Ginger,' they told him, offering my dad a huge weekly cash stipend to climb aboard their roller-coaster ride to terror and mayhem. (What his precise role in their world might have been has always remained a mystery, since his skills, by then, were very much deskbound. Maybe my dad had been a nifty fighter in his slimmer youth, but by now good living and booze were taking their toll and he was distinctly overweight and porky.)

'I knew what you'd say, Mol,' my dad told my mum, after he'd politely declined the kind offer, deftly claiming that The Old Man 'wouldn't be too pleased' if he quit their betting business.

No self-respecting East End bloke would cite their missus' opinion as a potential barrier to an opportunity to up the ante financially. But the solidly macho code of the Krays world understood all too well that upsetting The Old Man, who garnered formidable respect in all quarters, wouldn't be right. So Ginger was off the hook.

'There's no way I'd get that involved with those boys,' my dad sensibly concluded.

'Best to keep on their good side – from a distance.'

So that's how Molly and Ginger came to be invited to the Big Bash at The Barn, along with all the others that knew them, from a distance or otherwise. Of course, I heard all about it from my mum afterwards.

'There was every kind of food and drink you could think of, Jac, pastries, gateaux, smoked salmon, big dishes of fresh salmon, prawns, chicken, turkey, beef, I've never seen so much food in one place, not even at a big wedding,' she told me. 'And they had loads of waiters and waitresses running around, pouring drinks for everyone all night, the minute your glass was empty, it was incredible.'

The assembled company, like the food, had been eclectic. Clergymen and cops, writers, glamour girls and bank managers, costermongers, stallholders, bookies like my dad, one or two local bigwigs, hundreds of people had turned out to party with the twins. There was a band, and a crooner, singing mostly Sinatra. ('My Way' was sung at both twins' funerals.) The hosts, of course, didn't boogie on down. They just sat there, at their table, immaculately clad as usual, surrounded by minions, smiling and greeting everyone, a bit like visiting Royalty at a Command Performance. Like many of their big bashes, the party was an excellent example of skilful public relations: the lavish hospitality for which they were renowned gave their underworld exploits a sheen, a gloss that never quite faded.

My mum, introduced to them for the first time, even reported back that they were very respectful, even polite.

'It must cost thousands of pounds to put on a do like that,' she added wistfully. 'Yet Ginger says…they didn't pay a penny for ANY of it!'

Funny that. It was rumoured that even the twins' equally lavish, over-the-top funerals were never actually paid for. Though not so surprisingly, this story has been frequently denied. Rumours and denials. 'Twas ever thus…'

CHAPTER 24

WORKING GIRL

After six months at Southampton Row, I am out, clutching a piece of paper confirming that I have achieved Pitman shorthand speeds of sixty words per minute and can type at a speed of thirty words per minute. Within a week, I have been offered my first office job – junior shorthand typist at an oil company in Savile Row.

'They're American,' sighs the rather snooty agency woman at Brook Street Bureau, Mayfair, her hair swept up in an impressively slick blonde chignon.

'They need a junior. The boss keeps coming back from the States with extra work, so the senior secretary needs more help,' she informs me, reading out from the card she's plucked from a jam-packed box of similar job descriptions.

'The salary is seven pounds a week with two weeks' paid holiday a year. And you'll also be getting ten shillings' worth of Luncheon Vouchers every week.'

LVs, as they were known, were an important incentive for office staff in the early sixties. After all, it was less than a decade since rationing had ended. So the government saw it as a priority to ensure that every worker had a proper meal every day. The employer footed the bill for the vouchers, which were tax free; someone in the office would hand you the precious little book of paper vouchers each Friday, to use in exchange for your daily lunch at a nearby café through the next week. My first ever LVs were for two shillings a day, plenty enough to buy a sandwich, soft drink and Crunchie bar. (The luxury of having my own money at last meant far too many Crunchie bars were consumed before and after work in those first months. Result: a slightly overweight sixteen-year-old.)

Carrot topped, chubby faced with cropped hair but quite smartly turned out in my bouclé wool coat and Dolcis stilettos, I found it all a bit daunting at first, this adult world where you turned up on the dot of 9am, waited at your desk to be handed a task, usually dictation or copy typing from someone's handwritten scrawl, working on it until you were free to duck out for an hour on the dot of one. Then more of the same for another tedious three hours until you were released again, out of captivity, into the heady excitement and bustle of the West End and Mayfair.

Being 'up West' every day, people watching, checking out all the well-dressed business types strolling around the department stores, inhaling the glamour of posh Mayfair, popping in and out of the cafés, was infinitely more interesting than school and less frenetic and pressurised than Pitmans – but the downside was that in the office you had to behave carefully, be polite and watch what you said to the adults, a huge stumbling block for me, given my sarky teen rebel demeanour.

And as a junior, the kid in the office, I hadn't understood that the job also meant menial tasks like making cups of tea or coffee if required. (Coffee machines were still in the future at this point.) Since my domestic skills were zilch, I initially struggled to manage even this. And I deeply resented it, the spoilt child who never did anything for anyone. 'I'm not their bloody servant,' I'd whinge to myself in the tearoom, waiting for a tin kettle that never seemed to boil.

My immediate boss was a thirty-something dark-haired woman called Ruby with whom I shared a small office overlooking Savile Row Police Station. Ruby was kind, vivacious and took me under her wing immediately, explaining that she commuted daily on the Piccadilly line from somewhere called Ruislip and giving me the general rundown on what was expected.

'We do all the correspondence for Hank and look after him,' she revealed on my first somewhat bewildering day. 'I do the bulk of it but sometimes I'm so snowed under, I need a bit of help. Hank does a lot of travelling to the States, so when he's here you're expected to jump.'

She wasn't exaggerating. Without Hank, the day would pass easily enough. I'd be given a bit of copy typing, usually letters from Ruby's own scribble or there'd be a handwritten report to be typed up, complete with messy carbon papers that meant you'd usually wind up in the ladies, furiously scrubbing the ink off your fingers by lunchtime. In between typing, I'd make Ruby the odd cup of tea, waiting impatiently at my desk for the longed-for release hours of one and five pm. There was a black Bakelite phone on my desk, just like the one we had at home. It never rang.

So I didn't attempt to use it. And on Friday, just before lunch, a girl from accounts would come round with the little brown pay packets containing your week's cash. Pound notes. Bliss.

Lolly had also found a similar job, working round the corner in Clifford Street, for a firm of accountants. Mostly, we'd have blown our entire wage packet by Monday or Tuesday and have to nag for handouts at home to get to work until the next little brown packet arrived.

When Hank was in town, things changed. Hank was extremely tall and commanding, with an ugly college-boy crewcut, pretty much what you'd imagine an American oilman to be – a loudmouthed master of the universe who expected everyone to bend to his will – and you'd better be fast. (Think J.R. in *Dallas* and you won't be far off.)

Mysteriously to me, Ruby's demeanour would change when Hank was around. She'd be all flushed and jittery, get in extra early, stay late after I'd left. She'd also spend hours in Hank's office with the door closed, ostensibly taking important dictation, leaving me to fidget at my desk with nothing much to do, until she'd emerge, in a pink-faced tizz, to hurriedly hand me more work.

Sometimes it would be my turn to enter Hank's inner sanctum and sit opposite his big desk, taking more dictation, letter after letter delivered in his Texan drawl, though luckily, he didn't speak too fast and I'd manage to get all of it down.

After I've worked there a couple of months, Ruby asks me to do something different.

'Didn't you say you did French at Pitmans, Jacky?' she quizzes, handing me a piece of paper.

'Hank can't understand a word of this letter and he wants me to get it translated for him.'

'D'you want to have a try?'

With the help of a French/English dictionary, I manage to translate the letter, which thankfully isn't very long. But it's a rod for my own back. Very soon, every letter from France that arrives in Hank's massive pile of correspondence is handed to me, to translate and type up.

It's fractionally less dull than the routine letters, the messy carbon paper, the boring dictation, the clunky, inky typewriter ribbon that takes half an hour to change. It fills in the time. But Hank, king of all he surveys, doesn't want to leave it there. Oh no. He wants to nail the deal, get it sorted.

'Hank says if you want to go to night school and study French properly, the company will pay for it,' Ruby tells me one Friday afternoon.

'It's a good opportunity, Jackie. It means you could one day's work for the company as a translator.'

Que? *Moi*? A translator? Here I am in my first ever job, just sixteen, free at last, and they want me to go to night school?

'I'll ask my mum over the weekend,' I tell Ruby who seems to think this bodes well.

But I am just playing for time. I don't mind French at all – Lolly and I now regularly devour every copy of French *Elle* magazine when we can find one on the West End bookstalls because the fashions and the poised, groovy models are way, way ahead in the style stakes compared to anything we have here. And across the road, in Regent Street, we have discovered an oasis of Parisian chic: a branch of Galeries Lafayette, the big French department store; we're already eyeing up a gorgeous green leather handbag with a five-quid price tag. But I have no desire whatsoever to study, be a translator. I'm here, bored witless, typing in Savile Row because I want the cash every Friday, so I can spend it all on clothes in the exciting shops around me and hang out more often in the West End, a fast-moving, glamorous place of endless promise to a sixteen-year-old from Hackney. There's excitement, adventure here. I haven't had a taste of it yet. But I know it's here for me...

I do tell Molly about the offer. She's chuffed, ready to back me. 'See, Jac, I knew it. They can see what a clever girl you are.'

'Yeah but I don' wanna go to night school, mum. I've just left. I'm never goin' back.'

Molly, of course, tells my dad about this offer. He too is pleased and proud of his daughter, the nasty Stan incident now conveniently erased from his memory. Yet neither try to push me to seriously consider this idea, view it as An Opportunity, which it unquestionably is for a first-jobber. And so when I turn up at the office on Monday, I tell Ruby I don't want to go to evening classes to learn more French.

'Well, you can still do the letters with the dictionary,' she says sadly. 'Don't know what Hank will say when he gets back from the States.'

Hank says nothing. She just wants to keep him happy, pander to his every whim. Looking back, I'm pretty sure Ruby had a very big crush – or more – on her boss. To be American still carried a huge glamour quotient, mainly thanks to the combined forces of rock'n'roll, Elvis and now the super-charged Jackie and John F Kennedy in the White House, wowing everyone with a new type of high-octane Presidency.

In my innocence, of course, I couldn't see that to a post-war thirty-something Middlesex housewife, a Texan oil exec was probably as sexy and irresistible a proposition as a round-the-clock love-in with George Clooney might be to her equivalent half a century later.

After about a year, I quit the oil company through sheer boredom and switched to being a West End temp. Lolly does the same for a while. Yet my first job served one very good purpose: it showed me quite clearly that the adult world of taking dictation from boorish bosses and meekly serving them tea and biccies – something that goes against the grain whenever I have to do it – can't possibly satisfy my craving for stimulation, for excitement. This yearning for something undefinable isn't something I can verbalise. It is just an instinctive desire to get out there and taste or experience whatever the world has to offer me.

OK, so I've been growing up in Grotsville. My education has been cut short, not by poverty or a pressing need to earn money, but by my refusal to take study seriously. But that wasn't going to hinder me: if you like, that 38 bus ride from Dalston Junction to Piccadilly, price tuppence, journey time twenty minutes in those traffic-free years, was my entrée into the wider world way beyond Hackney. Lucky me for living so close to the action.

CHAPTER 25
A STUNT

My father was one of thousands of bookies who lined up for a licence to operate a legal betting shop in the summer of '61. By the year's end, there were over 10,000 new betting shops spread across the country. By all accounts, the new shop got off to a good start, though neither my mum nor I offered to visit the new premises in Harrow Place to take a look at it. The unspoken assumption was that it would be business as usual; the money would continue to roll in. Which it probably did at first, though I was far too distracted by my new life of earning money, working in the West End and going out at night, to pay much attention to the new venture – and what it might mean for us.

Nor were there any changes to my parents' routine: they continued to step out regularly, my mum dolled up to the nines, still meeting up with my dad's punters or cronies or at the odd party or bash, occasionally visiting my dad's brother Neville's house in the 'burbs. Their summer holidays were now taken at the Royal Albion Hotel, Broadstairs – my dad liked the nearby pub, The Tartar Frigate – and Dave the chauffeur had long gone; black cabs remained the perpetual mode of transport. Buying a small car, like so many people were starting to do, was not an option: it would mean a change in drinking habits, something Ginger never contemplated.

I got my first taste of foreign travel with Lolly that summer with a ferry ride to Ostend in Belgium and a few days in the nearby beach resort of Blankenberge. Lolly had been there the year before with her family and extolled its virtues. Alas, Blankenberge that August was frustratingly chillier than London. So we shivered and posed for photos on the windy sand dunes in our floral patterned swimsuits, wandered round the pier, eating portion after portion of crunchy Belgian chips served with mustard pickles, sharing a room at a cheap B&B and pretending to ourselves that we were finally having a 'grown-up holiday'. No boys came onto our horizon, alas. We were still too young to play pick-up games – though that would change quite soon. There had, of course, been some resistance from Ginger to the idea of me going away unchaperoned. But there was little he could do. I was earning and could pay for it myself, though I still tapped my mum for cash handouts on a regular basis.

At some point, my dad must have realised that the business wasn't doing as well as he'd hoped because later that year, he got involved in a Big Idea to get some useful publicity for the new betting shop. The idea would get him a photo, a big headline and a full page article in the *Sporting Life* newspaper, then the bookie/punter's daily printed bible, nowadays a website. He'd already appeared in the paper when opening the betting office because of his shop's ranking as the first legal betting emporium in the City of London precinct, a sort of feat when you consider all the illegal activity in the area in the past. But this article was a crafty publicity stunt, designed to bring in extra punters and more readies.

The idea was born after an extended session in the bar of the George and Dragon, with some creative input from one of my dad's regular drinking pals, a *Sporting Life* reporter called George and my dad's two big chums, Charley Riley and Mick 'Weasel' Douglas. Essentially, it was quite simple: 'Ginger Sid', the name my dad was known by in the Lane, would be dressing up as the Lord Mayor of London, with a gold-peaked black velvet hat, ermine cloak and chains of office chinking around his neck. Charley and Mick, the bookie's clerks, would be similarly dressed up in the Lord Mayor's Show ceremonial gear, complete with swords. George the reporter would write up the whole event and the mayhem it caused in the betting shop, tongue-in-cheek. A theatrical costumier, Bob Sand, another crony, would lend them the outfits – and, of course, get a mention in the article. Perfect PR. Pure theatre.
The story was duly written, with lots of East End 'colour'.

'Git darn 'ere to Petticoat Lane right away…either the Lord Mayor 'as tiken over a bettin' shop 'isself – or Ginger Sid's gone barmy,' read the opening paragraph of the story, which, to the writer's credit, read like a dream, describing in vivid prose the sight of Ginger Sid marching around outside the shop in his Lord Mayor clobber, doffing his hat, bowing at passers-by and generally encouraging locals from the Lane to venture into the premises.

''Ow much d'you want for that old chain?' quipped one old

man in a cap and muffler, dropping the handle of his handcart to stare at Ginger Sid's regalia. 'Give you eight and ninepence for it.'

'Excuse me,' said one old lady peering at the 'Lord Mayor's' tricorn hat. 'Why don't you wear your hat the other way round?'

'Cos then, madam,' snapped Ginger Sid, 'it would only serve to make me look sillier than I already do…'

Yet while the article and photo of my dad in his Lord Mayor gear appeared to much fanfare, the end result was seriously underwhelming: the regular punters still loyally called in at the shop to place bets. But no new business ensued as a result. My dad's customer base, as it is now known, remained pretty much what it had been before legalisation; extending it was not a simple matter.

Neither my mum nor I knew much of this, of course, beyond the article. Nothing was said about the real reasons why he'd co-opted the reporter to write up the stunt. But when the truth came out much later, it was clear the stunt had been born out of something very close to desperation.

My dad had run into trouble with his cash flow. So he did a bit of a Nick Leeson and gradually started using other people's money that wasn't his to use: from the bank, from his business partner, from the shop till, putting down big cash bets on the horses, in the hope of recouping his losses and re-establishing his finances.

In the first six months, one or two big bets came off. So he could keep the business going – and still keep betting. Over a period of two-and-a-half years, he was continuously playing hard in the last-chance saloon, placing bet after bet, juggling cash, copping the losses, convincing himself that a few seriously big wins or complicated bets would put him back in the black.

The irony was, my dad had never been much of a gambler himself; he'd have a bet now and again and that was it. But now his furious betting spree was destroying his business – and our livelihood. The business itself, inherited by Jack from his father, had stood in the Lane for well over a century, a tiny bit of local history. My dad managed to blow it all within a few years of legalisation, a time when economic optimism was high, there was full employment and consumerism was starting to change lives for good. Certainly, this was the Lane, the East End, Fagin territory, the traditional habitat of the chancer. People went bust all the time – and restarted again. But even by local standards, this was poised to be a spectacular cockup.

The extent of Ginger's borrowing remained undetected. Because he regularly operated an agreed overdraft facility with the bank, it was relatively easy to go back to his friend, the manager, and up the ante, borrow more. And because he and he alone operated the till of the shop – he had never quite trusted his counter clerk, Charley Riley, and his business partner didn't even come to the shop very often – no one could have a clue as to what was going on. Months passed and the debt was mounting. Yet everything went on as usual, my dad flashing wads of cash in the pub, downing double scotches and shouting doubles for all every night, still assuring my mum that we were living on 'the finest and the best'. No one knew a thing.

CHAPTER 26

WHAT'S IN THE BOX?

Office jobs in the West End were so easy to find and with my first year's experience under my belt, I could job hop with incredible ease. After a less-than-stimulating stint temping (the attraction of temping ended when the agency sent me for a soul-destroying fortnight at a big typing pool in Portman Square, akin to being on the production line of a factory, or worse, being back at college under the vengeful eye of Sister Brigid), I found it ridiculously simple to get a new job, sample it, leave after a few months of dictation and boredom and walk straight into another, usually via an employment agency. The agencies had so many shorthand/typing and clerical jobs to fill that it was a breeze for them to find work for virtually anyone with a bit of experience who came walking through the door. If you had decent speeds plus one good reference, that was plenty.

Sometimes you'd go for two or three interviews and wind up being offered every job. As a result, I was extremely casual about the whole idea of working. I'd grown up in a world of 'live for now' at home and was spending every penny I earned. Unlike many other East-End teenagers out at work, I was under no obligation to hand over a pound or two to pay my way at home. So seeking some sort of permanence or continuity at work just didn't come into the equation.

It was all far too easy. A job interview usually went along these lines:

'So…I see, Miss…er…Hyams, you can do Pitman shorthand and type at forty words a minute?'

'Yes I can.'

'Well, we certainly need someone like you to do our letters. We get a lot of correspondence and Mister so-and-So needs all the help he can get.

'When are you available?'

'I could start next Monday.'

'OK, next Monday it is. 9am sharp.'

This kind of 'speed hiring' sounds incredible now when three, even four interviews are not unknown for certain types of jobs. But there's a lot to be said for a world of full employment: the knowledge that another job is yours for the asking makes for a more confident worker, albeit a somewhat fickle one. And overall, office standards weren't that exacting: I was literate, could spell and did the work quickly. Often, the bosses giving you the dictation or handwritten letters had poor verbal or literary skills; you'd wind up discreetly correcting them on paper. And often, a secretary or typist was only there to boost their executive status. Frequently, you'd sit all day with absolutely nothing to do. The bosses didn't exactly run around tearing their hair out: it was, in office terms at least, definitely a more leisured era. Or maybe I just chose places that were a soft option.

I worked for an engineering association (as uninspiring as it sounds), a theatrical agent (too quiet: like the agent's clients, I sat there, waiting for something to happen but being paid; the ever-diminishing list of clients must have starved), a film distributor (interesting, at last, but long four-hour industry lunches made for tricky afternoons when my boss came back totally wrecked or the MD got amorous), and a fat, camel-coated, cigar-chomping Soho entrepreneur whose main income came from flogging cost-price table lighters and whose enterprise was run by a tiny, domineering woman called 'Hillie' – my first female boss and definitely not a feminist.

My key criteria for choosing a job was simple: the office had to be in the 'right' part of the West End, close to the 38 bus route and ideally in the streets around Soho and Piccadilly, which included a bit of Mayfair.

Soho, for Lolly, me, and a few like-minded Hackney girls we teamed up with, was the epicentre of our social world. Soho had all the places where we wanted to hang out: coffee bars like Les Enfants Terribles on the corner of Dean Street and Diadem Court and La Bastille on Wardour Street. These places had tiny basement dives, part of a growing number of small, smoky basement clubs like St Annes (near the church in Wardour Street) where you could have soft drinks and dance to records from the jukebox.

The overwhelming attraction of these places, of course, was the clientele: glamorous, dark-eyed, handsome young French or Italian boys, here ostensibly to learn the lingo, or work in the burgeoning catering trade – but primarily hoping to lighten the gloom of a greyer, colder clime by copping off with compliant young 'Eeenglish' girls.

The French were mainly bourgeois students with parents subsidising their studies. The Italians were mostly in London to work, complete with a work permit (back in those pre-EU days you couldn't get into the country without the right papers) that gave them a lower-ranking job in the posh hotels like The Savoy, enabling them to send most of the money back to their impoverished families.

Les Enfants was an early favourite. It was open in the day, and we could go there straight from work and on weekend afternoons when the best-looking Italian waiters were having their afternoon break before starting their evening's tasks.

These stunning-looking charmers with fractured English were infinitely more attractive to us than the local Stamford Hill boys in their baggy jumpers which had been knitted by their mums – think fried egg 'n' chips versus a tasty bowl of spaghetti Bolognese. Amongst our peers we were seen as a bit daring in rejecting our own 'manor'; as I've said, it was pretty much expected we'd pair off with one of our own kind. But in wanting to be 'up West' all the time, we were only following a pattern: living just a few miles from the centre, our families too had frequently stepped out there on special occasions as we were growing up, or taken us there on kiddie outings. (Molly already had a serious West End shopping habit going back to her wartime years selling underwear in Oxford Street.)

But there was a cultural shift going on too, something that started to emerge in those afternoons jiving at Les Enfants: a growing awareness of a certain kind of Eurocool. For kids like us, anything French or Italian – movies, fashion, as well as young men – was desirable, exotic, the youth more slickly costumed than the duller post-war Brit version. They may have been skint Italian waiters but the Latin passion for 'la bella figura' meant that many looked more like movie stars.

The swinging sixties, the miniskirted, long-haired, thigh-booted fashion and music explosion, when London became the global focus of cool, was still a few years away. Before that, the only really snazzy dressers in London, apart from the sharp-suited Mod boys, tended to be from across the Channel – and the only shoes worth buying were Italian. In Paris, straight-haired, full-fringed girls had been wearing skinny cotton pants, ballerina shoes and black T-shirts or polo necks à la Bardot since the late fifties. By now, we were aping the latest European looks, sporting bouffant hairdos, sleeping in rollers, backcombing and lacquering like crazy. But we didn't, couldn't, look quite as cool as they did.

We were East-End kids from a tough post-war environment. Yet being able to work around Soho meant there were no barriers to this, our further education: we could easily absorb and soak up some of the culture around us. Alongside our obsession with French *Elle* magazine, small groups of us went to see Ella Fitzgerald sing live, had our first-ever Chinese meal for five shillings in Shaftesbury Avenue, enjoyed Italian subtitled movies like *La Dolce Vita*, *Rocco and his Brothers* or Pasolini's unfathomable *Accattone* at the Academy, Oxford Street, jived to Ray Charles's 'What'd I Say' and 'Hit the Road Jack' at La Poubelle in Great Marlborough Street, or smooched up close with fanciable young Italian waiters to the strains of 'Georgia on my Mind'.

Soho has always been a melting pot of cultures, and a hub

for the sex trade. Yet it didn't feel threatening in any way; there was no sense of danger or menace wandering around those streets after work when we'd finished primping and preening in the plush ladies' loos of one of the big West End department stores, clicking down the stairs to the basement dives in our stilettos, atizz with anticipation, or heading to the Marquee Club on Oxford Street on jazz nights. The fact that many of our dancing partners spoke very little English only added to the excitement. In our small way, we were living dangerously, differently: it was all new – and therefore thrilling.

When the music stopped, we'd totter down Wardour Street to the number 38 bus stop, sometimes accompanied by one or two eager suitors. Occasionally they'd steal the odd brief kiss at the bus stop. But that was it: these boys lived in shared digs, two, even three to a room, so there was no likelihood of them trying to lure us back to their place. Even someone living solo in a bedsit was unlikely to risk incurring their landlady's wrath by bringing girls home. But if we did want to make a hasty escape, we'd occasionally splash out on a black cab back to Hackney, priced at eight shillings and ninepence.

That's if we didn't spot Lolly's dad, with his light on, going down Shaftesbury Avenue.

'Aargh, geddin you two and I'll bleedin' well get you 'ome in a flash,' Monty would say. And he did.

The summer of '62 sent Lolly and I on our first-ever package holiday: two weeks in the Italian Riviera at Diano Marina. We took our first-time flight to Nice, uneventful enough and an improvement on the lengthy cross-Channel ferry journey, and after a wait of several hours, a coach took us, via the dazzling and scarily winding corniche, across the border at Ventimiglia into Italy.

The resort was OK but a bit scrubby and disappointing. We'd expected it all to be a lot more exotic and mysterious, palm-fringed white sands and blisteringly hot days and nights. What we got was quite different: a series of concrete buildings, some quite new, a fairly narrow, crowded beach and our somewhat dreary hotel, catering mainly to package-tour Brits and a long long walk from the centre of Diano with its more interesting looking outdoor cafés and, hopefully, boy action. Who knew that Italian beaches were so regulated, and that you had to pay to use them? The weather, even in August, wasn't particularly hot or sunny. But we donned our striped swimsuits, as seen in French *Elle* (as usual, we bought exactly the same item in different colours) to splash around in the water, and plonked ourselves on our paid-for deckchairs: children, really, playing a grown-up game.

After a couple of days I am sporting huge mozzie bites on my arms and legs, which itch furiously. Yet nothing can dim our enthusiasm for actually being here, in Italy, the ultimate location in our quest for Good Boy Hunting. We even venture into a hairdressers and point and gesture to indicate what we want. When we emerge, the result, we agree, is far better than the somewhat floppy bouffant achieved in our local salon at home: this version is bouncier, higher, sleeker. Italian.

We quickly develop a routine: up late, trundle down to the beach by day, back to the hotel for the evening meal, usually a sparse plate of spaghetti with watery sauce or vegetables with a tiny bit of fish or chicken, followed by a big tarting-up and heavy backcombing session in the room before hitting the streets of Diano, heading for the coffee bars in town, wishing and hoping…

Our parents would have been horrified at our *modus operandi*; my dad would have had a heart attack had he known. Because what we are doing, quite deliberately, is nothing more than casually picking up, night after night, a series of different Italian boys who are hanging around, eager to make contact with pretty young foreign girls, chancing it, though our aspirations are going in different directions to theirs. We are still pristine, virginal, yearning for passion, romance of a sort with a glamorous local; they are hoping for a lot more action, even the Full Monty, than they'd expect to achieve with their own girls.

And yet…nothing bad happens. Incredibly, we are only too happy to jump into cars with total strangers, be driven around – even then, Italians adored their cars and showing off their country – and, in exchange for our company and the odd snogging session we conduct our own version of meet the locals, see the sights. It never gets out of control. No one tries to rape us, drive us off into heaven knows where to have their way with us. There's no booze, no drugs, no coercion.

Almost every night we meet another pair of boys, have a different kind of adventure, driving around the Ligurian coast, revelling in the delight and novelty of being young and carefree on warm summer nights in the Med; it's a new kind of hedonism for us, light years away from what we know in Hackney. A few of these boys speak some English but mostly we have to deploy our shaky French and the odd Italian word we've picked up along the way to communicate. We laugh a lot, muck around, tease and are teased; yet it's a bad night if we don't find ourselves, still laughing, being driven back to our hotel at an ungodly hour, waking up the stroppy porter, saying farewell to our latest conquests, whom we never see again. And we have a long-standing pact that we stick together, don't split up. This pact is what probably keeps it all safe.

Yet there are dangers involved in this game, beyond the sexual. We really don't know who these guys are that we are so happily picking up. How could we? We have no real knowledge or experience of Italy, other than a few blokes encountered in a Soho coffee bar, chosen for their sleek looks. We know Italians are still regarded warily back home.

'Eyetie quislings,' Ginger would sneer. 'Too scared to fight and didn't know which way to run when it got bad.'

'Bloody Fascists,' was cabbie Monty's view of the Italian race. 'Sucked up to 'itler and paid the price.'

We'd been hearing this stuff since we were kids. Yet Italy's wartime record didn't deter us one whit; it was ancient history, anyway. But one significant event made it clear that in our innocence, we were, in fact, playing with fire. Literally.

Tonight's two pick-ups are a bit older, early twenties. Normally, one tends to be more fanciable than the other. (The unfanciable one usually has better English, for some mysterious reason.) But tonight's duo, encountered in a crowded outdoor café, are both equally alluring, one quite blond, one dark haired: bandbox fresh white shirts, perfectly laundered by their loving mamma's hand, neatly pressed narrow cotton trousers, beautifully tanned, white teethed: we adore the way they look. And their English isn't bad.

'Why Engleesh girls so beautiful?' jokes Mr Blond.

'Cos English boys so ugly,' we quip back, happily accepting their offer of a drive around.

It goes on like this, in their car, for a couple of hours, Mr Blond driving, occasionally throwing one liners or longing glances at me, seated in the front (we're both in love with him, really) while the dark one, who obviously lives in the area and knows it intimately, directs him to a local beauty spot, some miles along the coast.

We are parked. It's about 1am and if it's romance you hanker for, you cannot fault this setting: a million stars twinkling in the sky above (a revelation to inner-city kids; we've never seen a sky like this), the glittering reflection of moon on the calm blue waters of the Med, the tranquillity of the soft, balmy air. There's a brief but heady silence. The dark-haired one puts his arm around Lolly. Mr Blond switches off the engine, smiles meltingly. Then, without knowing why, because I have never done this and am rarely inside a car, I reach out before me and open the glove compartment. And I cannot quite believe what I see inside the box.

It's a gun. A small, black handgun.

I stare at it in utter disbelief. At first, my words won't even come out. Lolly, peering behind me, sees the gun too. She too is terrified, scared to speak.

'What's a GUN doing there?' I finally manage, stupidly. What I should have done, for once in my life, was close the glove compartment and shut up.

But it's Mr Blond who leans across me and gently closes the glove compartment. He says nothing. The dark one pulls Lolly close and strokes her hair, murmuring something in Italian.

Unbelievably, Mr Blond is smiling at me, a sort of rueful, but forgiving look.

'Why a gun?' I try again (I always was one for pushing my luck).

He shrugs.

'Cosa vuoi?' Non è niente.'

Lolly and I know, roughly, this means 'Whaddya want, it's nothing.'

A gun? Nothing? What constitutes 'something' in Italy – a Cruise missile?

But the entire spell of the romantic moonlit setting, of course, is well and truly broken. Whatever intentions they might have had to woo us, they've been dashed by my reckless curiosity. Mr Blond makes an executive decision. He revs up the car and whoosh, we're off on a long, nervily silent drive back to our hotel for forty minutes, which seems like hours.

At one point, I pretend to fall asleep, nodding off, figuring this is a safe course of action. The dark haired one keeps his arm around Lolly, but makes no more attempts to kiss or nuzzle her. Later, Lolly tells me that she is so scared, all she can think of is what Monty would say, language unprintable, if he knew we'd stepped out with two guys with a gun in their glovebox.

'Ciao Jakka,' Mr Blond says as we stumble out of the car, relieved and thankful to reach the hotel door. Then, with a screech of brakes, they're gone, off into the soft, balmy Ligurian night.

In our room, we giggle about it as we throw off our shoes, undress and climb into our respective beds.

'Trust you, Hyams, to be nosey,' Lolly admonishes me.

'Yeah but who thinks they're gonna find a GUN in there?'

Within minutes, we are sound asleep. Our brush with the unknown, a lethal weapon, does not distress us. The next day, we don't even go through a 'What if' conversation about it over breakfast. It's just something else to laugh or joke about later on.

Even today, it's a riddle. Were those handsome young men hitmen for hire, baby Mafiosi, sun-kissed killers with white teeth and hip sunglasses? Or was it merely a toy, a joke? Somehow, I don't think so. My guess is, we were lucky; two silly young girls from Hackney could easily have come a cropper that warm August night. But thanks to the arrogance – and ignorance – of youth, we never waste a further minute's thought on what the contents of that glove compartment signified. Or if we'd been in any serious danger. At that age, you don't have the capacity to pause for serious reflection. Everything around you seems to hold far too much promise to concern yourself with worries about whether it might be risky to climb into a total stranger's car, at night, in a foreign country, at the tender age of seventeen.

CHAPTER 27
A FERRY RIDE

Easter in Paris, 1963: Eiffel Tower. The trio of teenage girls perched on metal chairs are smartly attired, sleek leather jackets (purchased for £20 from C&A), high backcombed hairdos, ski pants with stirrups under the feet. Lolly, Adrienne and I are on a three-day break, a long dreamed of chance to wander round the boulevards, admire the shops and soak up the beauty of the City of Light.

The trip is not a success. We have not budgeted for a capital city, naively using last year's Diano trip as a benchmark: surprise, surprise, the city is far too expensive for young typists. Our meagre allowance of French francs flies out of our hands with astonishing speed. Nor are there any friendly, amorous young Frenchmen offering to drive us around or buy us drinks. Paris is crowded, bewildering, its inhabitants mostly bad tempered and rude. Even our attempts in cafés to use French meet with classic Parisian derision: a sneer or a reply in English is the usual response, hardly encouraging to self-conscious teens.

Passports must be handed over to the hotel on arrival. The owner retains them – and studies the surnames carefully. So when we finally go to check out of our one-star hotel, in a seedy area, we come face to face with the ugly reality of Parisian post-war hostility towards foreigners – especially Jews.

We'd used the hotel's ancient phone to make reverse charge calls home, to assure our families we were alive and well, an added expense but, in my case, a necessary cost: it shut my dad up, briefly quelled his paranoia about what might happen to me Abroad.

The final bill, handed to us by the owner, a grim-faced, rude and intractable old woman, the classic snarly Parisian concierge, takes us aback. It's an enormous amount for two reverse-charge calls. It will clean us out, leave us without any francs for the journey home, several hours of near starvation and thirst on the train and cross-Channel ferry. So we query it, pointing to the total, making all the signs and gestures that indicate 'can't pay, won't pay'.

Our suitcases are in the lobby beside us. A nasty argument erupts. We yell in English, she bellows back in angry, rapid-fire French. We're being ripped off – and we know it. But we're kids and we don't know how to handle such a situation, far from home. So we eventually cave in, rummage around between us, pool our dwindling resources and grudgingly fork out.

But it's not the end. Without warning, once she's snatched our money, the woman waddles round from behind the counter, picks up our suitcases and proceeds to hurl them, one by one, out of the tiny lobby, chucking them out into the narrow Parisian street.

'Sale Juif!' she cries, as our cases hit the pavement. Dirty Jew.

'Sortez d'ici, salauds sales!' Get out of here, dirty bastards.

And then, to add insult to injury, as we run out to retrieve our cases, she moves to the hotel door and stands there, quivering with hatred. Then she spits at us, the ultimate street gesture of contempt.

We are bewildered, shocked beyond belief. She has obviously checked our surnames in the passports and noticed the Star of David that Lolly wears. She'll take our last penny. But she cannot tolerate the idea of our existence. We understand our history all too well. We know that some people, despite all that has happened, continue to hate Jewish people, want them all dead. But this open expression of hatred, the distant echo of what led to the slaughter of millions, is something we have never known. Only years later do I come to understand the dual nature of the French experience during the war, how some French people resisted the Occupation, while others supported the hunting down of Jews, and collaborated with the Nazis to do their worst work.

I don't tell my parents when we get home, of course. I don't want to say or do anything that might jeopardise any future travel plans. Nor does the incident make me wary of future travel, going abroad. But the incident is never forgotten, a brush, a glimpse of what could easily have happened to us, our families, our classmates, had we been born in the wrong place at the wrong time.

By now, my frustration with living at home frequently approaches a point of despair. Throughout that year, I am absent as much as is humanly possible and my weekend avoidance routine, either asleep in my room or getting ready to go out, mostly works. I hear my dad, of course, discussing things with my mum in their room. But my contempt for him and his way of life now knows no bounds. I've started to see a bit of the world around me and cannot understand why we must remain living in this awful flat, in this miserable street, when he has all that cash nestling in his pocket.

I never talk to any of the neighbours, even if I come face to face with them. I hate where I am. I thirst to escape. But I don't know how to go about it; I'm still too young to fend for myself, to find a path that takes me away from my environment.

Many young girls who seek escape from a less-than-happy home life find it in pairing off with someone. This never figures as a wish, a hope, even an idea in my thinking. I'm fixated by my attraction to men, worry frequently about still being a virgin, have occasional, fleeting crushes on some of the boys I encounter but am far too fickle and immature for anything beyond that. I only hunger for freedom itself. I don't want to hitch my star to someone else's life to achieve it and anyway, that wouldn't be freedom, would it? Round and round it goes in my head, the slow, painful, embryonic process of puberty, not a child any more, not really a woman yet. Emotionally, it's hell. I type, I dance, I flirt, I shop. But internally, all I really want, dream of, is to get the hell out of Dalston. For good.

There is a recurring nightmare I have time and time again throughout 1963. It started the year before, not long after the Cuban Missile Crisis, when the world hung on the brink of nuclear war, a brief but nail-bitingly tense standoff between the US and the USSR after the discovery of Soviet missiles, aimed at the US, in Cuba. Over a two-week period in October 1962, the conflict between Russia and the West seemed to put all our lives in jeopardy: would the Russians use their nuclear arsenal to attack the US? And would the US retaliate, and blow us all into oblivion in the process?

News travelled much more slowly then. Radio and TV reports were quite different, no 24/7 rolling news media as we now know it, no worldwide web; information released to the general public was much more tightly controlled. Day after day, as the crisis worsened, it was the newspaper headlines warning us of the threat of total catastrophe that we largely relied on to feed us the story. And so, as the crisis reached its peak, there was one unforgettable night when the entire nation went to bed wondering if we'd wake up to be told that the nuclear button had been pushed – or, indeed, if we'd even wake up at all. It was that bad.

My nightmare is always the same: I am in the flat with Molly and Ginger. It is quiet outside, eerily calm, and we are waiting. Waiting for the world to end, sitting in our lounge, staring at the slate roof of the building behind our living room, waiting for the nuclear bomb to drop. And I am trapped there with my mother and father, the life I am about to begin, the adult experiences I hunger for, now snatched from me forever by nuclear war. There will be no escape…

It's said that this was the closest the world ever knowingly came to nuclear war, so my fear, fuelled by a series of 'the end is nigh' newspaper headlines, is understandable. But to me, the dream demonstrates my deepest fear that I will never break free, that fate – or the unknown – will snatch my future from me. It's just a dream. But the effect on me is profoundly unsettling. When will I get out?

Two girls are sitting, somewhat dejectedly, on the upper deck on a cross-Channel ferry from Calais making its way back to Dover. It's September, the weather is already autumnal, the sea is choppy and the girls' somewhat sombre, flat mood matches the cloudy skies. Soon, they'll be back in grotty Hackney, going to the office each day, the excitement of their precious foreign holiday behind them for another twelve months. And, as usual, they are skint. All their lira have gone, mostly spent on strappy shoes and silky Italian tops from the local market. Tired, hungry and with that horrible end-of-a-good-time feeling they dig around in their handbags: just enough English money for two soft drinks to get them through the next few hours.

Lolly and I are on the return leg of a three-week trip to Pesaro, Italy, a resort on the Adriatic Coast. We've travelled by boat and plane because it's cheaper than flying –and allows us to have that extra week. We've had an OK, if uneventful time, chatting up the locals, being whizzed around by eager young Romeos keen to practise their English and, hopefully, improve their seduction techniques. But the holiday does not manage to recapture the lustre, the sparkle of the previous year's fortnight in Liguria. Could the attraction of Italy be starting to fade?

A fair, good-looking man in his twenties in a black polo-neck cotton top and white slacks strides by, glances briefly at the two girls, and comes back, wants to chat. They immediately brighten. Michele is a waiter at the Savoy, returning to London after a holiday visiting his family in Bari, right down in the south of Italy. Funnily enough, the girls vaguely recognise him as one of the off-duty waiters they know from the basement dancing at Les Enfants.

'You DANCED with him, Jack,' Lolly hisses at me later in the loo before the ferry docks, after Michele has very generously bought us all badly cooked chicken and chips. I hurriedly apply some pink lipstick. I know this guy's face from Soho – he doesn't really look typically Italian – but that's it.

'Don't you remember?' pushes Lolly. 'You came back afterwards and said, "What a miserable bastard."'

'Nah, don't remember. But I'm glad he bought us a meal, I was STARVING.'

We take the train back to London with the handsome, courteous Michele whose heavily accented English is nonetheless quite good. He's twenty five, has already worked his way up through the catering trade, learning it in Switzerland and Rome, a man of the world, who often misses Italy, his mama and his ten siblings. At Victoria Station, he sees us into a taxi, pushes a £5 note into Lolly's hand. 'I call you,' he promises, having carefully taken note of Lolly's number.

We sit back in the cab, pleased with ourselves for having cadged a final meal and ride home out of one more Italian charmer. Michele's attentiveness has brightened up the end of our holiday.

A couple of weeks later, Lolly and Michele are engaged.

A week after we get back, he rings Lolly briefly, suggests we both meet him for coffee at Les Enfants before he starts his evening shift. There, he invites us to a party in Victoria the following weekend.

'Italian boys 'ave a small party,' he tells us. 'I take you there.'
We nod eagerly. Italian boys. Party. Right up our street…..

At the party, we are the only girls. Four deeply unattractive
Italians are lounging around, noisily debating god-knows-what
in Italian. The shabby flat boasts a small record player and Rita
Pavone is belting out 'Cuore' (Heart), the love song heard on
every jukebox in every Italian beach resort that summer.

I survey the unappealing flat feeling distinctly deflated.
Nothing here for me. Not even any grub. By now, it is
obvious that Michele is after Lolly. On the somewhat battered
sofa, he has his arm around her, is whispering sweet nothings
into her ear. I am a tad annoyed. He may be after Lolly but
he's lured me here on false pretences. Why didn't he just ask
her out? So I stomp out, hail a taxi and head for Dalston.

The next day, Lolly rings me, unhinged, flustered – but
smitten beyond belief. Michele has proposed!

'He took a ring from his pocket, put it on my wedding
finger and said, "This my gran' mother ring. I wan' us to be
engaged." Then he kissed me; it was incredible. So romantic.
And then…someone took a photo!'

Wow. Could it get more like a fairy-tale romance? You meet
a handsome, dashing young Italian on a boat, after a few
weeks he proposes – then he kisses you for the first time ever
as someone records the moment for posterity. Incredible.

'What you gonna do?' I query.

'I dunno. I'll just have to see…my mum and dad will go
mad…he's gorgeous, though, isn't he?'

Early in '64, Larraine, her hair piled up in fantastic coils,
wearing a stunning knee-length white feathered coat dress
from Galeries Lafayette, stands on the steps of Hackney Town

Hall with her handsome new husband, Michele. Later, they have a wedding feast, mostly prepared by Michele, now Mike, at her parents' flat. I am working, so can only join the celebration that evening; wearing in my new blue crepe trumpet-sleeved dress I join her family and friends to wish the newlyweds well, toast them with champagne. Yes, there was quite a lot of carrying on and shouting when Lolly told her family she'd fallen for Mike. But somehow they've shelved their prejudices and warily accepted the newcomer.

I am thrilled for my friend, dazzled by the glamour of the reckless whirlwind courtship. And, without even acknowledging the shift in tempo, now that my best friend has signed a piece of paper to show she's an adult and has moved into Mike's tiny bedsit off the Earl's Court Road, I too am soon reaching out for adulthood – and my first ever lover.

He's a cliché, a hero delivered straight out of Mills & Boon, dark, skinny, utterly charming and meltingly dashing, and found on the dance floor at the Whisky a Go Go in Wardour Street. Paolo is twenty six, from Ferrara, not a waiter but a wealthy Italian medical student in London for a few months to improve his near-perfect English. Green eyes. Leather jacket. I fall for his physical charms pretty quickly. He doesn't have to do much to convince me either: intuition tells me this is it. I'll willingly throw all caution to the wind and lose my virginity to this man. For by then, I am desperately eager for the experience itself. While we were still emerging from an era of 'nice girls don't' unless they're engaged, semi-hitched, there was no way in the world I was about to allow the conventional wisdom to curtail my need to find out more about sex, life, you name it. Unable to swim, I dive in headlong anyway.

But of course, the first time isn't always a passport to ecstasy. Leaping into Paolo's arms, after a slow courtship (about a week) mostly spent after work in or on the tiny bed in his little studio flat in Holland Park, building up, bit by bit, to the big event, until we finally go All The Way, isn't quite the intensely passionate earth-shattering experience I'd been reading about in trashy American novels since my early teens. It's exciting, no question. And it is only, briefly, painful. But the whole thing has been marred somewhat by medical student Paolo's terror of getting me pregnant. So our lovemaking is a case of coitus interruptus. Paolo refuses to use a condom, though, of course, even using the hit-and-miss method meant I still risked pregnancy.

'You have Pill in England, no?' he'd asked me when it was obvious, after the second date, where it was all heading.

'Yes but I can't get it,' I told him and it was true. The Pill had been available on an NHS prescription since 1961, but I'd heard the prescription came from your GP and there was no way the family doctor in Dalston would have given me the precious piece of paper. So my first time, like many, was far from ideal. But…I'd done it!

'He's going back to Italy next week so I don't know if I'll see him again,' I tell Lolly over the phone.

'I'm SO pleased I've done it. But I wanna do it again… with someone else.'

'Are you sure, Jack?' says Lolly, unable to conceal her shock at such calculation. 'I thought you really liked him. He sounds like he really likes you.'

She's right. Paolo is attentive, affectionate and is talking about coming to see me again in a few months' time. But with the fickleness of youth, my mission accomplished, my period on time, I don't particularly want to be Paolo's girl. We talk on the phone. But I avoid seeing him again. And so he returns to Ferrara, no doubt pleased with his conquest. But somewhat puzzled by the behaviour of these strange English girls.

CHAPTER 28
A PLAN

For once, I actually like the new job: secretary to the sales manager of an electronics company off the Tottenham Court Road. The company market innovative new products: telephone answering machines, which can only be rented out on an expensive five-year leasing contract. This is no easy sell, so the company employ freelance salesmen or agents to market the machines, paying the agents £100 per sale, a huge sum for those times.

The place is swarming with hungry salesmen, all ages, motormouths with fast patter, keen to chat up virtually every woman on the planet – especially the girls in the sales office, me and my colleague Denise. This is much to do with our close relationship with the sales manager, Mrs Burton, whose husband is one of the company bosses – and partly to do with the ultra-fashionable short skirts we are wearing.

The miniskirt was now in danger of taking over central London, giving every red-blooded man a daily peepshow of flesh to ogle, a distraction that is fast transforming the daily commute, the office grind.

Today it would be labelled harassment, men in the office commenting endlessly on how you look, how they fancy you, how they can see your knickers if you bend over to retrieve a piece of paper. We called it having a laugh, giving as good as we got with a saucy retort or a well-aimed insult. Many modest girls held back, of course, sticking to the primmer, longer hemlines. But those, like me, who instantly adopted the 'pelmet' look, took the attention for granted.

I'm well paid too. That's because there's a hidden bonus. Me and the switchboard girl, Brenda, have struck a deal with one or two of our favourite salesmen: if we get a hot lead, a phone call from someone saying, 'I want one of those answering machines straight away', we take down the details and immediately pass them on to Favourite Agent. In return, once the deal is sealed, we get a cut of the commission, £30. It's all top secret, of course, though Mrs Burton probably guesses it's going on and doesn't really care provided the sales figures are good.

Enjoying my job, the daily banter with the agents, the not-so-subtle flirting with the cheekier ones, the extra cash (it all goes on clothes), I'm also moving into a different social sphere: I've acquired a boyfriend, Bryan, met one warm August night in the De Vere Club, Kensington.

Bryan works in an advertising agency in town as something called a copywriter and drives around in a souped-up Mini. His parents live in Wimbledon, his dad is 'something in the City', but Bryan rents a flat with a friend in St John's Wood. He's pretty worldly, four years older than me, totally unlike anyone I've met. He's not a toff. But he's so obviously much posher than any other English boy I've known, I can't fail to be impressed by his savoir-faire.

He takes me to riverside pubs, out for Indian and Chinese meals, and drives nervily fast. He also plays the drums sometimes in a jazz band. On the looks front he's not in the same league as the beautiful Italian boys – a bit tubby, a bit slobby, no matter how fashionably expensive his gear – but his charisma somehow draws me in. After a brief, intense courtship in the back of the Mini, we finally consummate the relationship in his flat one weekend when his flatmate is away. After that, if his flatmate is around, we sometimes wind up making love in the car; uncomfortable, yes. But exciting, too.

Sex with Bryan is fast and furious, usually fuelled by drinks beforehand in the Bull and Bush or The Spaniards, though unlike Paolo he always carries 'a packet of three'. Sometimes, as he drives me home to Hackney, speeding like a maniac, he'll light up some 'weed', the word used to describe cannabis or dope back then. The smell is strong, heady. But I won't try it. I'm too scared by the idea of drugs.

Bryan makes it very clear that he is not in the least impressed by my surroundings, my background. If he picks me up at home, he toots the horn impatiently in the car downstairs, as if he can't stand to spend a minute longer than necessary in grungy Dalston. He won't come up and say hello to my parents. I don't encourage him to do this, naturally. But surprise, surprise, Ginger develops an intense loathing of my new friend. He insists, time and again, that he knows what Bryan's all about, what he's after.

'He's using her, that bloke,' he tells my mum repeatedly if Bryan rings me and I rush to the phone.

'He won't show the respect, come up here, he's just bloody using her.'

He meant, of course, that Bryan was 'using' me for sex. And though I hated him for being so vocal in his view, he had a point. Swinging London was, by now, poised to be the focus of the world, a combination of the phenomenal success of bands like The Beatles, the Stones, the soaring youth culture on the streets and the explosion of design and creativity coming out of the capital.

Yet it still wasn't that simple, on the cusp of all this change, for an average-looking guy with a car, a good job and a flat to find a willing, young attractive girl to take out and about, be a regular bedroom partner without the rituals of going steady followed by an engagement ring. East-End girls my age still either lived at home or moved out to marry. We were at the very edge of the sexual revolution. But it hadn't happened yet. And sure enough, after the initial few months when Bryan and I see each other two, three times a week he changes tack, starts calling less often.

'I'm not ready to settle down,' he tells me. 'So it's up to you if you want to keep seeing me.'

In my heart of hearts, I wasn't that naive. The guy wanted to have me around, mainly for sex, when it suited him, and to keep his options open, see what was available elsewhere: pretty standard male opportunism really. Of course I wasn't entirely comfortable with this – I wasn't exactly sophisticated – but I was hooked on the excitement, the challenge of Bryan, the fast car, the posh pad, the sex – and the fact that he was a bit racy. The regular, steady guy was never going to keep me interested. So I made a decision. I'd play the same game. I certainly wasn't going to sit around waiting for Bryan's call. I too would be out and about.

This combination of having a regular, if erratic lover and earning good money proved to be the turning point I'd yearned for. At twenty, I'd finally reached the point where I could actually see my way out of Dalston. My big idea was to find a flat share, somewhere good in green, leafy north-west London, which I'd already acquired a taste for. I could afford to pay rent and I'd finally have my freedom…

I don't say a word of my plan at home. I don't even mention it to Bryan, whom I now see about once every few weeks. This about-turn in the relationship would have been seriously upsetting had I not been so preoccupied with my exciting escape plan. I start scanning the classified ads in papers, checking out rents for shared places. Within a couple of months I have found exactly what I want: a big, two-bedroom flat on two floors above a shop in Hampstead. I go along to meet the three girls I will share with, all from the provinces, working in London. My share of the rent, £4 a week, is affordable. My roommate, Angela from Manchester, is bright, lively and full of fun. We agree I'll move in within a fortnight. A bright new world away from Dalston is opening up to me, just as I've dreamed.

But what I don't know then is that another world is about to collapse, for ever…

CHAPTER 29

SHE'S LEAVING HOME...

The front door to the flat is wide open. It is mid-afternoon, Saturday, and I am finally going, taking just one suitcase with me. It contains all my worldly possessions, my clothes and shoes, packed that morning once I'd heard the front door slam behind my dad as he makes his way to the Lane.

My mum knows what I'm doing. I've primed her a few days before.

'I don't blame you, Jac,' she tells me sadly.

'You can come back if you don't like it, you know that.'

I want to tell her I'm never ever coming back, not under any circumstances, but her face is so miserable, so forlorn, instinct stops me from blurting this out as I'd normally do. My dad will be told tonight, after I've gone.

'He's been so funny lately, I don't know how he'll take it,' my mum says, shaking her head.

'But there's a phone in the flat, isn't there, so he knows we can get in touch with you if we need to.'

'I don't want him ringing me, mum. I'll ring you, I promise,' I tell her.

We're so selfish when we're young. I have no inkling how painful this all is for them, losing me, their adored only child, watching me walk away.

Guilt, for me, at hurting her doesn't even come into it. I have wanted out of this place for so long. I am blind to anything but my overwhelming need to separate, break the cord.

And so she sits in an armchair, watching me, trying to hold back the tears, as I go through the door, suitcase in hand, all the love in the world unable to stop me from doing what children must, eventually, do. Yet while I have a powerful desire for independence, I am not in the least prepared to fend for myself, either emotionally or in a practical sense. I cannot cook, have never cleaned, beyond a bit of washing up and am not used to sharing my life in any sense.

But leave I must. The practical issues will take care of themselves.

As I step outside, go to close the door, I hear my mother sobbing her heart out. It is a pitiful sound but, to my eternal shame, I do not look back. Down the stairs I go, lugging my case. Bryan, who has recently been told my big news, is waiting for me round the corner in Shacklewell Lane to take me to the new flat. My case just about fits into the car and we're off, speeding down King Henry's Road towards my future, away from the only world I've ever known – and cannot wait to put way behind me.

'A girl like you should have her own pad, eh Jax,' he says at the traffic lights, reaching out to briefly caress my cheek, a rare sign of affection – other than when we've just had sex.

'Does this mean we'll see more of each other?' I snap artfully.

'Who knows, kiddo, who knows,' he says glibly, a typical Bryan response.

'How about a quick drink at the Flask once we've dropped off your case?'

Three weeks later my mum rings me unexpectedly at the office. She has something important to tell me. Can she come and see me today in the lunch hour?

That day, she sits in the tiny café opposite the office, smart as usual in her navy blue suit, black patent handbag and pearl earrings and tells me exactly what has happened.

'Your dad has lost his business, Jac. He started gambling heavily. I don't know when, but once he started, it all went wrong. Thousands of pounds. He's had to sign over the business to his partner. But he's come away with nothing. A good job I'd managed to keep a little bit of money, it'll just about get us through a couple of months. He owes the bank thousands too, but he seems to think he'll get away without paying them back.

'It's terrible. I don't know what he'll do. He keeps saying he's relieved it's all over. But at least you're OK, Jac. I'm so relieved it's happened now, now you've moved away.'

I stare at her for a minute. It takes a while for it to sink in. Then we reach out simultaneously to hug each other hard. She doesn't cry, like she did the day I left. She's just her usual normal self, brave, uncomplaining, putting me first as usual. At the entrance to my office I promise her I'll come over on Sunday. I don't want to go there. But it's all I can do.

I dread Sunday but my fears are groundless. Ginger is sober and rational. He talks quite openly about his crash.

'Once you start laying out for the big bets, you can't stop; it gets a hold on you. It was too much for me, running that shop. Everything's changed now, anyway, now it's legal,' he says ruefully. 'Only the big boys can make it work, you need a chain of shops, not just one.'

Incredibly, the bank have agreed to wipe the debt; they won't be chasing him for the unpaid overdraft of several thousands of pounds.

''S'pose they know it's not worth trying to get money out of someone who's totally boracic,' he tells me.

He's spot-on there: Ginger's lack of belief in mortgages, savings, insurance policies, jewellery or any form of asset have, in reality, saved him from Carey Street (the old nickname for being in serious debt or bankruptcy, named after the street near Chancery Lane where the bankruptcy court once stood). There's nothing at all for the bank to retrieve, just a cash-only business with an oft-raided, now empty till.

I don't tell him I'm sorry. I'm sorry for my mum but my loathing for how he's been over the years is still strong; he's brought all this on himself, I tell myself later. But a week later brings a surprising breakthrough. My mum, ever resourceful, has gone down Kingsland Road to visit her old employers, Jax at Dalston Junction, on the off-chance there's work there. And yes, they need Molly's experience selling lingerie and underwear, the new pantyhouse now replacing the rapidly going-out-of-fashion nylon stockings. Can she start next week?

And so, the years of plenty, the big wad of cash, the endless bunging, the big nights out with the punters, the chauffeur-driven holidays, Wag, the human Ocado, the 'have it now', loadsamoney world of my parents' post-war years finally ends.

My mum is grateful for the chance to work, to save my dad. Her earnings won't be anything like what they had before but will cover their costs, feed them, keep the roof over their heads. My dad, bewildered by the loss of face, stunned by the reaction of his former friends, most of whom vanish, and confused at no longer having his self-employed status, stays at home, relieved that they can survive, that the slate is clean, at least. He still goes to the local, round the corner. But he's pretty sober now. He can't afford more than a drink or two.

As for their daughter, I am far too taken with my new sense of freedom, already peering round the next corner, hankering for the next adventure, the next discovery, to concern myself for too long with what has happened.

But who can blame me, a miniskirted, curious twenty-year-old girl living and working in the heart of the most happening city on the planet? They say the sixties didn't really happen for you if you can actually remember being there. I too cannot remember all of it; there was too much going on, especially in the late sixties. But I can assure you that when I reflect on what I can remember, one thing is abundantly clear: it was a very, very good time to be young, free and female in Swinging London. Wherever you'd started out from.

Afterwards

Following his fall from grace and for the first time in his life, my father, aged fifty-three, found a steady job as an accounts clerk at the British Medical Association. He worked there for ten years until ill health forced him to retire. He died, following a stroke, in 1981.

My mother, widowed at sixty-five, found a new partner in due course and eventually moved from our 'temporary' home in 1990. She died in 2009.

As for me, after a hectic few years travelling around Europe, working on and off in a variety of different types of jobs, I left to see the world. In Sydney, Australia, I started writing, initially as a features writer for *Cosmopolitan* magazine, then as a columnist for *Rolling Stone*, *The Sydney Morning Herald* and a host of mass-market publications. Always restless, after many years overseas, I returned to London and forged a successful, long career in journalism as a magazine editor, newspaper columnist, bureau chief and author.

And even now, all those years on, I still hold the opinion that Italians are the best-dressed men on the planet...